Quiet De...

Alaska's
Empty
Chair
Story

Karleen Grummett

for

The Empty Chair Project

Library of Congress Control Number: 2015914907

ISBN 978-0-9679182-1-1

Book cover and layout design by Sarah Olsen, Sarahgraphics, *sarah@gci.net*

Empty Chair Memorial Design by Peter Reiquam, *preiquam@hotmail.com*

The *Juneau* print is from an original painting by, and courtesy of,
John Fehringer, *www.johnfehringer.com*, *art@johnfehringer.com*.

Printed by A.T. Publishing & Printing, Inc., Anchorage, Alaska.

The Empty Chair Project, *www.emptychairproject.wordpress.com*

*This project was funded, in part, by a grant from the Department of the
Interior, National Park Service, Japanese American Confinement Sites Grant
Program. Any opinions, findings, and conclusions or recommendations
expressed in this material are those of the author and do not necessarily reflect
the views of the U. S. Department of the Interior.*

*This material received Federal financial assistance for the preservation and
interpretation of U.S. confinement sites where Japanese Americans were
detained during World War II. Under Title VI of the Civil Rights Act of 1964,
Section 504 of the Rehabilitation Act of 1973, and the Age Discrimination
Act of 1975, as amended, the U.S. Department of the Interior prohibits
discrimination on the basis of race, color, national origin, disability or age in its
federally funded assisted projects. If you believe you have been discriminated
against in any program, activity, or facility as described above, or if you desire
further information, please write to: Office of Equal Opportunity, National
Park Service, 201 Eye Street, NW (2740), Washington, DC 20005.*

ACKNOWLEDGEMENT

Quiet Defiance: Alaska's Empty Chair Story focuses on the years 1941 to 1951 and those Japanese Americans who were forcibly removed from and those who returned to Juneau during that time. However, the Empty Chair Committee wants to also acknowledge those who were not living in Juneau then, but whose families were similarly impacted.

CONTENTS

PREFACE

Anti-Japanese sentiment had been building on the West Coast of the United States for quite some time before the bombing of Pearl Harbor on December 7, 1941. It had taken an ugly turn with the adoption of The Exclusion Act of 1924, which prohibited further immigration by people of Japanese descent.

Those already in the country were forbidden by law to become citizens or to own property in California, Oregon and Washington. In these states, Japanese immigrants, the Issei, either leased property or had their children, the Nisei, who were U. S. citizens by birth, purchase property for them. Alaska, then a territory, did not have such property restrictions for immigrants.

Following America's entry into World War II, a combination of prejudice and war hysteria engendered an unprecedented action by the United States, before or since, when President Franklin D. Roosevelt issued Executive Order No. 9066 on February 19, 1942. The order effectively created the framework for the military exclusion, forced removal and incarceration for all people of Japanese ancestry, nearly two-thirds of them American citizens, from the Pacific Coast comprising the Territory of Alaska, the State of California, the western half of Oregon and Washington and the southern third of Arizona.

Miné Okubo, who published the first personal documentation about the incarcerations, wrote, "The

United States Army took charge. Within three weeks, race tracks, fairgrounds, and parks were made over into assembly centers. Within three months, 110,000 (this number was subsequently adjusted to 120,000) people of Japanese parentage were moved from their homes."

They were sent to ten incarceration camps: two in Arizona, two in Arkansas, two in California, and one each in Colorado, Idaho, Utah, and Wyoming. In addition, U.S. Department of Justice camps held 3,000 Japanese aliens considered potentially dangerous by the Federal Bureau of Investigation.

All were imprisoned without being charged with a crime or due process. The camps were placed in isolated, barren locations surrounded by armed guard towers and barbed wire. Stunned and confused, they didn't know where they were going, and they didn't know if they would ever return.

The majority of Alaska's Japanese Americans (some 200) were taken from communities in the Southeastern part of the territory. Thirty-five of them were from Juneau. Understanding the scope of Japanese treatment and incarceration during World War II requires acknowledging the unique and personal experiences of Japanese Americans, which rarely include those living in Alaska. This book begins to rectify that omission by narrating the lives of Japanese Americans in Juneau, Alaska, when it was a small, tightly-knit and remote community accessible only by boat. This restrictive environment, where people instinctively relied upon each other, played a key role in their reactions to this traumatic episode of the town's history.

What unfolds is a story about those Japanese Americans living in Juneau between 1941 and 1951, how they reacted to their forced removal from Juneau in 1942, how their spirit and resolve helped them live during their imprisonment and how they renewed their lives following it. The story also describes how the Juneau community's cross-cultural ties and friendships rallied support for their missing friends during and after incarceration, and how those circumstances led to a quest for justice more than 70 years later.

INTRODUCTION

Juneau, the capital of Alaska, sits along the West Coast's northernmost temperate rainforest in the state's panhandle. It rests sheltered between the green intensity of the imposing Mt. Juneau to the north and Mt. Roberts to the east, their flanks studded with narrow, hilly streets filled with colorful vintage homes. In front, Gastineau Channel laps the shoreline separating Juneau's mainland from Douglas Island. Wharfs, boats and floatplanes dot this marine setting where government and tourism lead the area's economy for more than 30,000 citizens and where the cement, bunker-styled State Office Building surveys the town's vistas from Telephone Hill.

By contrast, at the turn of the century, though fishing was central to Juneau's economy, gold had been discovered in 1880, and the community was primarily a rustic mining town of only 2,000 people. Homes sat among tree stumps left from earlier clear-cuts, and it was the Federal Courthouse atop Telephone Hill that punctuated the landscape. Alaska was a district of the United States then, and Juneau had become its capital in 1906.

Across the channel, the Treadwell Mine was operating in Douglas, and in 1912 when Alaska became a territory, two more companies began operating mines on the Mt. Roberts portion of Juneau's mainland. The Alaska Gastineau Mining Company's mill was operational by

1915 and the Alaska Juneau Gold Mining Company's in 1917, the year a cave-in shut down the Treadwell.

During this evolving period in Juneau's history, its economy attracted a variety of immigrant cultures, primarily Slavic and Scandinavian, pursuing dreams of a more fulfilling life. But a smaller group of these adventurous souls from Japan also shared this dream.

PROMISE

Living in Juneau, it is not unusual to experience quiet winter Sundays with snow muffling sound and flakes settling lightly on spruce needles. In 1941, when the population of almost 6,000 was concentrated downtown, it wasn't so quiet. The roar of floatplanes taking off in Gastineau Channel joined the constant bustle of a town centered on the 24/7 activity and shifts of the Alaska Juneau Gold Mine, the largest low-grade gold mine in the world. Its huge mill hung from Mt. Roberts, and a line of miners' head lamps, like a string of fireflies, were visible as workers trudged up the mountainside trail during late or early shift changes.

On the Sunday morning of December 7, 1941, with the temperature hovering in the mid-20s after two days of snow, 14-year-old Tom Fukuyama headed for the Douglas Island Ski Bowl with Mack Mori and Haruo "Ham" Kumasaka, a certified first-aid member of the ski patrol. Ham drove the delivery truck for Tom's father, owner of the Juneau Laundry, and for whom Mack worked as its tailor. After some vigorous ski runs, they began walking home across the bridge connecting Juneau with the island. Ham said that's when they learned that Japan had bombed Pearl Harbor. "All hell had broken loose in town," he said. "People were panicking because the only way out of Juneau was by boat."

Dean Williams, another avid skier, was driving across the bridge with a ski group that included a Japanese American friend when they heard the news on the car radio. Williams said, "After that, it was very quiet the rest of the way home with everyone thinking their own thoughts. It was a complete shock." When Tom, Ham and Mack got back to the laundry, Tom's family had already heard the news, wondering what it all meant.

Juneau's Early Japanese Community

That December day would have been unfathomable to future Juneau proprietors Shonosuke Tanaka and Hikohachi Fukuyama when they sailed into town forty years earlier. The Japanese immigrant population then was composed of men primarily working the mines, restaurants, laundries and outlying canneries. Most were bachelors. Two pioneering families, Bunzo and Tsuyu Makino and Matajiro and Yaso Kanazawa, were the exception. Matajiro ran a barber shop, and the Makinos, whose daughter was the first Japanese child born in Alaska, ran a variety store on Front Street. Due to illnesses and deaths, these families would return to Japan in the 1920s, with the exception of the Kanazawa sons, Tooru and Torao.

One of the bachelors, Shonosuke Tanaka, immigrated to the United States in 1900 seeking a better life as a contracted worker for the Northern Pacific Railroad. He eventually moved on to Seattle where he took English classes and employment as a kitchen helper, an experience that exposed him to Western recipes and formed the foundation for his life's occupation. Aptly prepared, he journeyed to Cordova, Alaska, where he started his first café that fed locals and workers from the Kennicott Copper Mine. When the mine declined, he moved on to Juneau and opened the Star Café in 1907.

By 1912, Shonosuke had relocated to South Franklin Street. The move coincided with the startup of the Alaska Gastineau Mine's mill, about five miles further south on Thane Road, and the Alaska Juneau Gold Mine's mill across the street and down a few paces. Perhaps thinking the miners would be a good source of customers, Shonosuke centered his new restaurant, which he called the City Café, smack in the middle of the town's core

Young Japanese men, ca. 1920. Top row far left, Tooru and Torao Kanazawa and far right, Usuke Hamada; second row 4th & 5th from left, Shonosuke Tanaka and George Miyasato; front row left, Hikohachi Fukuyama. Children: Harry & Mary Makino.

industrial activity. The boat harbor, with fishermen offloading their catch was a few yards away, as were the local saw mill, steamship docks and boarding houses. The Alaska Gastineau would eventually fold in 1921 leaving the Alaska Juneau mine as the town's major gold producer.

Takashi Kono, delivering takeout, 1940.

Shonosuke's leased, two-story building featured a front counter with a kitchen at the back in one section, a room with curtained booths in another and rented rooms on the second floor. Shonosuke's new, bustling restaurant served hearty, generous meals at reasonable prices to miners, longshoremen, mill workers, fishermen and businessmen from a varied menu featuring sourdough pancakes, halibut cheeks, roast beef, chow mein and boiled tongue. Many miners turned in their lunch pails at dinner to be washed, placed on a shelf, refilled with thick roast beef or pork sandwiches and picked up the next morning.

Saburo Tanaka and Torao Kanazawa, ca. 1930s.

Shonosuke presided over an assortment of bachelors who included waiters Torao Kanazawa, Takashi Kono and Saburo Tanaka (no relation to Shonosuke). Takashi, with his slicked-back hair and swagger, was quite a contrast to the constancy of Torao and the reliability of tall, soft-spoken Saburo. As for their employer, Shonosuke didn't suffer fools, but he was a fair, honest and reliable employer who produced substantial, working men's meals every day. Torao's brother Tooru, who later wrote the semi-biographical *Sushi and Sourdough* based on his Juneau experiences, provided this account of Shonosuke's demeanor. "He was a large-framed Japanese," he wrote. "Though he was fleshy, his pounds were so well distributed he did not look fat, nor had they warped his straight back. His large eyes beneath heavy eyebrows were shrewd and appraising. Those close to him knew he was not to be trifled with. His jowls could not hide the fine lines of his strong jaw," which contrasted with "a normally pleasant expression." Whatever his demeanor demonstrated, it began attracting regular customers to his new restaurant.

In due time, Shonosuke purchased a home on a patch of hillside near the Carrol Way stairs not far from the cafe. His good friend Bunzo Makino and family would live on the first floor, and another friend, truck farmer Toraichi Toyokawa, cleared the area behind it for a garden, terracing the gentle slope with rock walls.

Tanaka home on Carrol Way.

Then in 1922, Shonosuke, now 40, returned to his Japanese village, Buzen-Shoe on Kyushu Island, and married Nobu Fujita, 19, in an arrangement by their two families.

Upon their return, Nobu began adjusting as a newlywed and immersing herself into a very different culture and language. She created bountiful flower and vegetable gardens with Toyokawa, who helped her cultivate the land each year. Nobu's rural background in

Japan most likely instructed her knowledge for enriching the soil with local organic matter, like manure from a local dairy and ashes from her stove, to produce vegetables like onions and Swiss chard for the restaurant and flowers she enjoyed sharing with others. Toyokawa was viewed as a kindly uncle to all the Tanaka children, who would ultimately include John, William "Bill," Teddy, Alice and Mary.

When it came to the café, Nobu, whom everyone took to calling "Mama," eventually became responsible for renting the upstairs rooms to café workers, miners and longshoremen. Her daughter Alice Hikido referred to Nobu's upstairs area in the restaurant as "Mama's Kingdom" where she also kept a room among the linens for entering ledger accounts in Japanese. Alice remembers spending time with her in those quarters, watching as Nobu cleaned the rooms and changed the sheets.

City Café, ca. 1938: Originally built as a boathouse by Norwegian fisherman Ole Orsen, it was remodeled & later leased by Orsen to Shonosuke Tanaka in 1911.

"She was a hard worker," she said. "And even though her English was limited, she was able to convey her goodwill to customers."

At the urging of a relative living in Juneau, Hikohachi Fukuyama came to Juneau around 1906 via a stop in Canada, first working in the Treadwell Mine on Douglas Island before becoming a houseboy for District Judge Royall A. Gunnison. There he learned English and cooking skills from Mrs. Gunnison. Eventually he moved on to work in the Juneau Laundry, which had been operating since the turn of the century, and by 1917 he owned the business with two other Japanese men. Three years later he sailed to Seattle to meet his bride-to-be, Mume Iida from Chigasaki, Japan. Like Nobu and Shonosuke Tanaka, Hikohachi and Mume's marriage had been arranged by their respective families. They wed, returned to Juneau and started their family of four children: Mary, Ethel, Walter and Tom.

By 1923 Hikohachi had become sole owner of the laundry, one of four such establishments in Juneau, and he and Mume immersed themselves in running the business. When he was ready to buy property for constructing a laundry building on a section of Franklin Street near the town's north-side neighborhoods and businesses, John Reck of the First National Bank facilitated the loan Hikohachi needed to achieve his goal.

Juneau Laundry under construction, 1929.

When it was completed in 1930, the family moved from their rental home across the street and into the cement structure's top floor lodgings for family and workers.

The City Café and Juneau Laundry soon became the main employers anchoring the small Japanese community, which included

Juneau Laundry interior, 1929.

Juneau Laundry exterior, 1930.

two notable bachelors working for the laundry: Ham and Sam. Haruo "Ham" Kumasaka, came to Juneau in 1939 to replace Tooru Kanazawa, who was leaving his job at the laundry for a journalism career. Ham told documentary filmmaker Greg Chaney[1] that Hikohochi Fukuyama sent him $25 and a steerage ticket to fill the job as delivery truck driver for the laundry. There he joined Mack Mori, the accomplished tailor who had moved to Juneau in 1936 and lived above the business with other bachelor workers. Alice remembers him as a "feisty, fun guy" who delighted children with Christmas gifts each year.

John Reck, Juneau's 9th Mayor, managed Alaska Meat Company & became president of the First National Bank. (ASL P14-43)

Mack Mori, 1940.

When a washing machine operator position opened, Ham contacted his friend Isamu "Sam" Taguchi in Seattle, who took the offer and moved to Juneau. Sam and Ham knew each other from growing up in the Green Lake area of the city and playing sports in its Japanese leagues. Sam's father died

The Taguchi family of Seattle. L. to R. Reiko, Gim, Matsuye (mother), Sam, Kimi, and Susumu Taguchi, 1944.

when he was in grammar school, so as the eldest, taking on responsibility to financially assist his family came

---

[1] Greg Chaney videotaped several interviews for his documentary film *The Empty Chair* during 2013. Alaska Japanese historian Ron Inouye assisted with those interviews.

early. Now it would include sending half of his laundry salary home. His sister Reiko said Sam would later help her with college expenses, too, saying he was very generous in that way.

Ham Kumasaka, Juneau Laundry delivery truck driver & friend Max Lewis with mitt, 1940.

Though the laundry workers lived in rooms above the business, they ate most of their meals at the City Café. "We could eat anything we wanted on the menu," Ham said. "Three meals a day for $1." Shonosuke often served his customers in other ways, too. He was known to provide loans for those who were down and out, and he let regulars run a tab for their meals when they were unable to pay.

Ham and Sam soon involved themselves in Juneau life, playing on the Elks baseball team and bowling for the laundry's team. "Sam was very knowledgeable about sports and very smart," Ham said, and Reiko said Sam's love of sports, both as player and later as coach, was a big part of his life. One of their teammates was Max Lewis, who had

Juneau Elks Baseball Team: Fifth from left: Ham Kumasaka and Sam Taguchi. Third from right, Max Lewis, 1940. Above, inset: Ham & Sam in Elks uniforms, 1940.

followed his sister to Juneau. Max and Ham were kindred spirits and became even better friends.

In addition to sports, Ham said, "The Lutheran Church was quite important to our social life." He and Sam enjoyed boat rides, picnics, dancing and ice skating with the church's young adult group led by Pastor John L. Cauble until 1941 when Reverend Herbert Hillerman arrived. One of the group was Katie (Torkelson) Hurley, the daughter of Norwegian immigrants, who was also a classmate of Ethel and Mary Fukuyama. Katie told Chaney of Ham and Sam, "We did dance a lot," she said. "They were very popular." Sam was also a friend to the Tanaka and Fukuyama children, sometimes taking Walter Fukuyama bowling or for some rounds of pool.

Hillerman, 1940.
(Courtesy Tim Hillerman)

Pastor John L. Cauble, 1941. (Courtesy Tim Hillerman)

Katie Torkelson Hurley.
(1939 *Totem* yearbook)

Ice skating on Auke Lake: Sam Taguchi, Ross Vories, Emma Nielsen Houston & Ham Kumasaka, ca. 1940.

The Fukuyamas

On some Sundays when the laundry closed, the Fukuyamas and their workers enjoyed picnics and berry picking excursions or watching baseball games from the stadium on the field where the current Federal Building now sits. Sometimes they drove 17 miles north of town along the lone gravel road, colloquially called "out the road," to Tee Harbor for fishing with Mr. Takisaki, a commercial fisherman. On even rarer occasions, the young families enjoyed special outings with the Tanakas and other Japanese American friends. However, the Tanakas and Fukuyamas seldom had time to visit each other because of their work, with one special exception. That's when Mume and Nobu stayed up late on New Year's Eve to prepare special Japanese foods like mochi (pounded rice cakes). Nobu also prepared makizushi made with seasoned rice and ingredients like spinach and sweetened egg omelette rolled into a sheet of seaweed. Then on New Year's Day, workers from the laundry and café visited both businesses to feast and celebrate their traditional

Outing with Mrs. Tanner and daughter, 1930. In front: Walter Fukuyama. Behind L. to R. Ethel Fukuyama, John Tanaka, Mary Fukuyama. Third row: Nobu Tanaka w/baby Teddy, unknown, Louise Tanner, Mrs. Tanner, Mume Fukuyama. Fourth row: Hikohachi Fukuyama w/baby Tom, 3rd from him is Torao Kanazawa and Shonosuke.

11

Young Japanese families on an outing to Salmon Creek, 1926. L. to R. first row: Ethel & Mary Fukuyama, John Tanaka, George Makino. Row two: Nobu Tanaka, Mume Fukuyama, Tsuyu Makino, Harry Makino. Row three: Hikohachi Fukuyama, Juneau Laundry owner, & son Walter; Shonosuke Tanaka, City Café owner; Toraichi Toyokawa; Bunzo Makino; Mr. Osumi.

holiday together. Nobu continued making makizushi after the war, and Mary liked watching her mother as she worked over the delicacy. "She seemed so happy as she sang Japanese songs," she said.

While the laundry business hummed along, at home, Mume stayed up late many nights mending customers' socks. "In spite of her busy day," Ethel wrote in *Gastineau Channel Memories*, "she always had time for us children." That included reading to them or sharing Japanese children's stories, sometimes drawing pictures as she went along. To give Mume a break from the kitchen, Hikohachi cooked Sunday meals that often featured his coveted rolls and pies.

Mume managed to save some time to enjoy a special friendship. "In spite of my mother's language deficiency, she and our neighbor, Mrs. Mead, used to chat away as they walked up the street together to attend PTA meetings," Ethel told Carol Hoshiko of the Japanese Pioneers Project. "You could call them an odd couple since Mrs. Mead, of Swedish extraction, was tall and big and Mama was tiny. Every time they could attend, Mrs. Mead always stopped by and picked up Mama and off they would go, Mama slowly running to keep up with Mrs. Mead." Likewise, Mrs. Mead's children, Bernice and Herb, were friends with Mume's children, too.

The Fukuyama children abided their required piano lessons, summer laundry chores and Japanese lessons from Utaka Kazama, known in the Japanese American community for the high level of education he had acquired in Japan. But in their free time they hiked to popular fishing creeks, attended birthday parties and joined in Saturday talent shows at the nearby Capitol Theater. Though the Fukuyamas lived far away from the Tanakas at the upper end of Franklin Street, the children were close in age and frequently played together, sometimes taking ski trips to Douglas Island.

Utaka Kazama, Japanese language teacher, 1950.

Walter especially enjoyed the outdoors, like ice skating on Auke Lake located twelve miles out the road. He told Chaney that he used a .22 rifle his father gave him for hunting grouse and ptarmigan, and when he could, he fished for trout. "It was like a Huckleberry Finn life. We'd go down to the docks and watch the fishing boats come in," Walter said. "My mother would allow us to go up the mountains. They wouldn't tell us what to do.... Growing up in Juneau was a magical time. It was a good place to grow up for a minority."

Walter was simultaneously sent as a goodwill ambassador from Juneau's Junior Chamber of Commerce to the boys and girls of Japan when his family visited Yokohama, Japan, in 1937. Back in Juneau, Walter and his siblings, like the Tanaka

L. to R: Tom Fukuyama, Bill & John Tanaka, 1938.

children, attended the white plastered, three-story public grade and high schools located side by side two blocks up from the laundry. There they contributed their energies and talents to many high school activities. In 1939 during her senior year, Mary played intramural sports, became president of the girl's rifle club, and served as secretary of the "J" and photo clubs. After graduation, as was the custom for the eldest Japanese child, Mary moved to Tokyo for her secondary education where she lived with relatives and began attending the prestigious Waseda International

The Fukuyama Family, 1938. L. to R. Ethel, Hikohachi, Tom (front), Mume, Walter & Mary.

School. However, Walter said Mary had a difficult time adjusting to the formalities of a woman's role there.

Mary Fukuyama. (1939 *Totem* yearbook)

Her sister Ethel, now a senior, showed talent as a member of the Quill and Scroll Honor Society, rifle club and the basketball and archery teams. Following graduation, Ethel focused on business school in Seattle. When she returned to Juneau in 1941, her youngest brother, Tom, was 13 years old, and Walter was a sophomore, playing on the basketball team and enjoying ski club along with teammate John Tanaka.

Ethel Fukuyama. (1941 *Totem* yearbook)

The Tanakas

As the City Café became a thriving eatery, the Tanaka children also thrived and, like the Fukuyamas, they enjoyed friendships made in scouting, church and school events. They were also encouraged to maintain a connection to their Japanese culture. Hakuio Inouye, a café worker, taught the Tanaka and Fukuyama boys the classical art of Kendo, a Japanese form of fencing with two-handed bamboo swords. The Tanaka children also studied the Japanese language with Utaka Kazama, who taught them in a small, one-windowed structure at the edge of Nobu's garden the Tanaka's called the Ba house. Also used for other pastimes, a basketball

Hakuio Inouye, café worker, taught Kendo to the Tanaka & Fukuyama boys, 1940.

The Tanakas inside the City Café, 1938. In back left, Shonosuke and John Tanaka. In front, Alice, Teddy, Bill and Nobu Tanaka.

hoop was attached to the structure, and John used it as a darkroom to develop photos for himself and school publications.

John was industrious in other ways as well. Alice described her brother for Chaney as "a very traditional oldest son. He was dutiful and reliable, all those things that probably parents would want in a first child." Her brother Bill was two years younger than John. "He came into the world with a different set of genes," Alice said with a fond laugh. "He was kind of rascally." She said that of the children, she and Bill were the most strong-willed, "We both remembered Mama's concern for our rebellious natures and the discipline that she

L. to R. Ken Thibodeau, Walter Fukuyama and Jack Pasquan. (1941 *Totem* yearbook)

frequently applied to us," she said. However, Nobu was not the sole disciplinarian in the family.

In later years while reminiscing about his childhood, Alice said Bill enjoyed telling a story about playing baseball with a friend.

Bill Tanaka, above, ca. 1939; left, ca. 1940.

When their ball landed in a neighbor's yard, the neighbor wouldn't give the ball back. "My brother probably had a little sense of justice," Alice said, "so he picked up some rocks and broke the neighbor's window." This resulted in a trip to jail for Bill requiring Shonosuke, still in his cook's uniform of white hat and apron, to

City of Juneau, ca. 1930s, showing the AJ Mill on upper right with South Franklin below. The street becomes Thane Road to the right, just past the mill site, & follows the shoreline left into the hilly downtown & the Juneau Laundry. The bldg. still remains. The City Café was just to the left and below the mine. (ASL P97-0075, Trevor Davis photo)

The Helpful Merchant: Emery Valentine

During the time Hikohochi and Shonosuke were establishing themselves in Juneau, the Japanese immigrant community was befriended by Emery Valentine, a merchant interested in Japanese culture. According to Trevor Davis in his pictorial *Looking Back on Juneau*, Valentine established a jewelry store in 1888, pioneered the Juneau Volunteer Fire Department and served as mayor for several terms. Shonosuke noted Valentine's interest. Alice said, "My father said that sometimes a Japanese worker would leave debts behind when leaving town and that Mr. Valentine would pay the debt. In this way, the honor of the Japanese immigrants would not be tarnished by the debt. I know my father really respected Mr. Valentine, and we always had his portrait in our living room."

Shirou Fujioka wrote in his book *Footprints of the Past* that around 1922 a Mr. Miyata, who worked in Valentine's jewelry store, initiated an effort to have Valentine appointed as honorary consul of the Japanese Empire for being a friend of Japan and for helping many Japanese immigrants

Emery Valentine, Juneau businessman and two-term mayor, receives Japan's Emperor's Medal for supporting Juneau's Japanese Community, 1922. Left in second row holding baby: Hikohachi Fukuyama. Next to him is Shonosuke Tanaka with a child in front of him. Front row (left & above children): Nobu Tanaka, Mume Fukuyama, Tsuyu Makino holding George Makino, Emery Valentine.

in Juneau. Shonosuke's efforts in this regard are noted in Fujioka's piece as being "very great." As a result of the two men's efforts, Valentine was not only appointed Honorary Consul of Japan for Alaska, but was awarded the Fourth Kuyoko-jitsu-sho Emperor's Medal (Fourth Class Order of the Rising Sun).

City of Juneau, ca. 1930s, taken from Mt. Roberts looking northwest. Landmarks: The Federal Court House, far left, on Telephone Hill; the Federal Bldg. (largest bldg. middle left); the white Juneau High School & Juneau Public Grade School, which burned in 1972. The grade school space became Capital School Park, & the Juneau High School became Capital Grade School & later the Legislative Affairs Bldg. South Franklin runs right of the grade school, & the Juneau Laundry is in the block far left just out of frame. (AKSL Trevor Davis Collection P97-0050)

fetch him. "I'm sure he got a licking, because my father was really a disciplinarian," Alice said. "I think there was a little of my father in Bill. I think my father may have been a rascally person when he was young."

Still, she remembers her father affectionately as someone who worked very hard "I didn't know anybody who worked as hard as he did," Alice said. "Maybe 14 to 15 hours a day, seven days a week." She once asked her father why her family couldn't spend Christmas together like other families. "But where would the customers eat?" he replied. "I never felt he thought that operating his restaurant was a drudgery," she said. Sometimes the family did manage an outing from work, such as visiting Toyokawa's truck farm located north of Juneau and watching, entertained, as his trained bear cub drank beer from a bottle.

Like the Fukuyamas, the Tanaka children found many outdoor activities to entertain themselves. In winter, they coasted on sleds down a hill behind their house. Whenever possible, Teddy practiced his fascination and skill for playing marbles outside with his friends. He was quite good at it, assembling a growing collection he stored in Nobu's sewing machine drawer. Alice was two years younger than Teddy, and sometimes he let her tag along to watch his games and even carry his marble bag home for him. "I was like his little shadow. I think he must have been aware that I looked up to him and thought of him as a special big brother," Alice wrote of Teddy in a memoir.

Toraichi Koyatawa, truck farmer and landscaper, with his trained bear, 1930.

She also liked to explore the side of Mt. Roberts with Teddy. "We would walk on the miners' trails and follow little brooks and streams that came down the mountain," Alice said. "It was the perfect playground, and we enjoyed such a time of innocence, having no thought of danger." But danger surfaced on a June day in 1939 when Alice did not accompany nine-year-old Teddy as he went off to play with friends, and somewhere along the way, he vanished. Though townspeople searched the area's mountains and waters and the family offered a reward for information about his disappearance, Teddy

Teddy Tanaka, far right, with friends Keith Weiss and Jack Sorri.

was never found. Alice said the family believed he may have drowned, possibly from a fall off a nearby dock, forbidden territory since the children didn't know how to swim. "Teddy's disappearance was so hard for us, and as a family we didn't seem to know how to comfort each other because we each felt so much pain," Alice said. "Mary's birth (in 1940) saved us."

Two years later in the fall of 1941, John Tanaka was a senior and academically slated to become class valedictorian. Despite that focus and his duties at the café, he was full-on engaged as a member of the math and photo clubs, student council, Quill & Scroll and the student newspaper staff of *The J Bird*. He also served as yearbook editor of the *Totem* along with his friend and associate editor Skip McKinnon, whose father operated the Alaska Laundry and

John Tanaka.
(1942 *Totem* yearbook)

Cleaners. Because there wasn't enough money available to publish the annual that year, John and Skip approached their fathers, who agreed to help fund the project. John's brother, Bill, served on the student council as sophomore class president and played on the wrestling and basketball teams. Alice was eight and little Mary 18 months.

Quill and Scroll

Standing: Skip MacKinnon, Harry Sperling, Dean Allen, Erling Oswald, John Tanaka. Sitting: Zaida Carlson, Pat Olson, Susy Winn.

John Tanaka with Quill & Scroll members. (1941 *Totem* yearbook)

Meanwhile, after school and on weekends at the cafe, Shonosuke and Nobu taught their children what amounted to a life skills training camp. Bill and John peeled pots of potatoes, washed dishes and waited tables during lunch hour. In fact, all the children acquired restaurant responsibilities from the time they were little. Alice feels that's where she got her best education as she and her siblings learned the value of respecting customers, working together for the common good and finding satisfaction in doing their tasks well. Shonosuke and Nobu modeled the value of hard work for them, and life was good.

BETRAYAL

Juneau's close-knit community had seen quite a bit of growth as a capital city since the arrival of the Fukuyamas and Tanakas, especially with construction of the new Federal and Territorial Building and the steel-girded bridge connecting Juneau with Douglas. In addition, the art deco-styled Baranof Hotel had opened in 1939 across from the Juneau Laundry, and an airfield was being developed in the Mendenhall Valley nine miles north of town, complementing the budding floatplane service. Adding to the town's promise, steamship visitors reflected an uptick in tourism and commercial fishing, and the Alaska Juneau Gold Mine still flourished. That promise must have lent an extra element of disbelief when the news of Pearl Harbor's bombing arrived that snowy morning of December 7, 1941. Like a tidal wave gaining speed, it quickly saturated the shocked, small town.

Sam and Ham's friend, Katie Hurley, who had begun working for Governor Ernest Gruening in 1940, was

L. to R. Katie Hurley, governor's office stenographer; Governor Ernest Gruening; Estella Draper, Gruening's secretary, ca. 1941. (Courtesy of Katie Hurley)

playing the organ at the Lutheran Church that Sunday when she heard a phone ring in Pastor Hillerman's office. After the service, an usher told her that the governor's secretary, who was known to use strong language when the occasion called for it, had left a message for her to call. The secretary told a stunned Katie, "Get your ass up here. We're at war!" At the time, messages between the military and the governor were sent in code. "I was the keeper of the code," Katie told filmmaker Greg Chaney. "I was the only person besides the governor who knew that this code existed." Katie's presence was needed immediately for communicating with Fort Richardson Army Base in Anchorage.

None, however, were affected by the news of Japan's betrayal like the town's Japanese American community. When Tom Fukuyama, Ham Kumasaka and Mack Mori arrived back at the Juneau Laundry after skiing, Tom's family had already heard the news of the bombing. Ethel Fukuyama learned of it as soon as she arrived home from church. "I couldn't believe it," she told Hoshiko. "And neither could dad. He said, 'It can't be.' But then, it turned out to be true." Ironically, Tom was a newsboy for the *Daily Alaska Empire* and was called in to deliver a special edition announcing America's declaration of war.

Walter Fukuyama told Chaney, "I guess that was probably the saddest day of my life up until then." He said he didn't feel right about Japan bombing the United States, although the kids at school didn't bother him about being of Japanese ancestry. However, he said, "A lot of good customers stopped (coming) when the war started." He added thoughtfully, "My father always believed in the American way, and he hung his flag on the Fourth of July."

Alice Tanaka's school experience was quite different. She felt apprehensive about attending class the next day. She told Chaney that after reaching her room, "It took only a few insensitive words by a classmate before I put my head down to hide my tears." She said the teacher told the class that Alice had nothing to do with the attack. Many years later a former student in that class, Marilyn Riggs Rudy, told Alice that she also cried, and when she told her mother what had happened at school, she cried, too. "This trauma affected everyone," Alice said. She told Chaney, "All of a sudden you are so aware of your ethnicity. Even though I was only nine years old, I was fully aware that I was Japanese and was different in that way."

Following the bombing, punitive action in Juneau was swift. The next day all male Japanese immigrants suffered the humiliating experience of being arrested by the FBI. Hikohachi Fukuyama's business friend Simpson MacKinnon, owner of the Alaska Laundry and also a Navy reservist, was sent with the FBI to search the Tanaka and Fukuyama homes before the arrests. Walter told Chaney, "He (Mr. MacKinnon) felt sorry for my Dad, but those were orders, and he had to do it." The FBI agents were thorough, searching through closets and kitchen drawers. Jeanne Tanaka, John Tanaka's widow, told Chaney the FBI grilled John for so long about his photography files that Mr. MacKinnon thought it had gone on long enough. "Mr. MacKinnon put a stop to all of that," she said.

James Simpson "Sim" McKinnon.
(Courtesy J. Simpson McKinnon family)

MacKinnon's grandson Neil MacKinnon told a *Juneau Empire* reporter in 1990 that Simpson was proud of his role during the war, but he always regretted the government's roundup and incarceration of Alaska's Japanese American citizens. "He knew these people and tried to keep them out (of incarceration camps)," he said. Alice said of the search, "Fear was really present for all of us." But they were aware of the awkwardness Simpson felt, too, because his son, Skip, and John Tanaka were friends. Simpson, Alaska's first U. S. Naval Academy graduate, would return to active military service as chief of staff for the 17th Naval District directing the World War II effort in the Aleutians.

Ham and his friend Max Lewis were members of the National Guard. Ham told Chaney, "The FBI came to me because I was in the military, and they wanted me to spy on the Japanese people." They went to Sam, too, he said. "But they didn't get any cooperation from me or Sam." The workers felt watched, however. Ham said an unfamiliar man began coming to the laundry every

Ham Kumasaka in his National Guard uniform, ca. 1938.

day to ask what they were doing. It was obvious to the employees that the stranger, who was a recognizable newcomer in the small community, was seeking clandestine information.

Following their arrests, Shonosuke and Hikohachi were taken to the imposing Federal Courthouse and its jail on Telephone Hill. Alice remembers her family's visit to see Shonosuke. "The Fukuyama family was also there," she said. "My father and Mr. Fukuyama were brought in together, and I remember a very subdued, constrained visit. Mrs. Fukuyama was quietly crying. My mother was fearful and apprehensive, although my father was making an effort of telling us not to worry." Christmas would be a very bleak occasion that year for the Tanaka and Fukuyama families.

Federal Courthouse and Jail, ca. 1920s. (ASL-P104-004)

Then on January 9, 1942, Shonosuke was arraigned in Juneau before a board of three civilians: Attorney Norman Banfield, Gastineau Hotel Manager Wilbur Wester and Territorial Employment Service Director Joseph Flakne. They would determine whether Shonosuke should be interned as an "enemy alien." The board called only one witness, George Hanrahan, an FBI agent who questioned Shonosuke about letters he had sent to Japan, the contributions he had made to organizations there and the money he had sent to his family.

Shonosuke remembered a few instances that could have been misconstrued as subversive following the panic of the Pearl Harbor attack. For example, Alice told Chaney that Japanese mining officials had once visited

Juneau to tour the AJ mine, and Shonosuke had hosted a meal for them. The FBI said they knew he had gone to the dock to say goodbye to the officials. "What did you hand over to the mining official at the dock?" Alice said they asked her father. Shonosuke didn't know what they were talking about then, but later remembered he had given the officials photographs taken around Juneau. At the time, Shonosuke thought they would make good souvenirs for the visitors. He later told Alice that the questions he was asked at the hearing indicated he had probably been under surveillance years before the war started.

At his hearing, six witnesses were called by Shonosuke: Cash Cole, manager of Cole Transfer; D. B. Femmer, manager of Femmer's Transfer; John Hermle, owner of Home Grocery; J. F. Mullen, banker; Douglas Mead, carpenter; and Shonosuke's son John Tanaka. Femmer and Mead gave no judgement about Shonosuke's loyalty to the United States. But Cole said he had known Shonosuke since 1908 and in his opinion, "Tanaka has more interest in the United States than in Japan."

Cash Cole, ca. early 1920s. (ASL Cash Cole-1)

Mullen testified that he had experienced business dealings with Shonosuke for 20 years. He said, "Tanaka's reputation for honesty and veracity is above reproach," and he believed Tanaka to be loyal to the United States. Mr. Hermle had known Shonosuke almost as long. He testified that he saw him daily in their business

J. F. Mullen, B. M. Behrends Bank president, ca. 1958.
(Courtesy of Anne Gruening family).

transactions, and that he was "honest, hardworking and a good business man." He said that he always thought Tanaka to be a loyal member of the community and was loyal to the United States.

The description of John Tanaka's testimony by the FBI agent focused on his volunteer work as the "official photographer for the Totem, official high school annual" and said, "He is an avid camera fan and is a member of the high school camera club." John told the board that most of the pictures he took in and around Juneau were of scenery and that his father had never asked him to take pictures. All the supporting statements were to no avail. Based on FBI evidence, the board determined Shonosuke "carries on activities which are adverse to the welfare of the United States, with persons known to be working for Japan." He would be incarcerated as an enemy alien and sent away. The hearing process and subsequent findings were also conducted with Hikohachi Fukuyama resulting in the same decision.

The prisoners were first sent to Fort Chilkoot in Haines, Alaska. Many years later in a taped interview with his son Tom, Hikohachi outlined the experience of their journey from Haines to the Department of Justice prisoner of war camp for Japanese aliens in New Mexico. Upon arriving at Fort Chilkoot, Hikohachi said, "We thought we were to be executed, shot by a firing squad. The commander came and told us not to worry. The soldiers will look after us." One of those soldiers was Japanese American Pat Hagiwara from Ketchikan. Years later, Hikohachi told his granddaughter Nancy Albright that, even though he was guarded with a rifle, he felt safe as long as Hagiwara was doing the guarding.

Hikohachi said the group was next sent to the Fort Richardson Internment Camp in Anchorage after it was built in February. From there they endured a long journey to Department of Justice camps in Tacoma, Washington; Texas; and finally, Lordsburg, New Mexico. Within the contiguous United States, the prisoners traveled by railroad. Hikohachi told Nancy that the train rides occurred at night with the windows covered, so they never knew where they were going. When they eventually disembarked in New Mexico, they were walked in the dark for approximately three miles, armed guards on either side, before reaching the Lordsburg camp. Along this same walk, two physically compromised Japanese men, lagging behind, were shot and killed by a lone guard, the only witness, in the early morning of June 27, 1942. Because some prisoners from Juneau were processed later that same day, according to Lordsburg historian Mollie Pressler, they were most likely part of the same group debarking from the train as the men who were killed, although most were already at the camp when the shooting took place. The names of Shonosuke Tanaka,

Hikohachi Fukuyama & Shonosuke Tanaka at Lordsburg, NM, prisoner of war camp, ca. 1943.

Hikohachi Fukuyama, Henry Akagi and Torao Kanazawa were among those listed as processed that day.

Meanwhile, the families had other concerns. Mume worried about how the laundry business would continue without her husband. "It was suggested that everything be transferred over to mother's name," Ethel told interviewer Carol Hoshiko. Attorney Mike E. Monagle helped the Tanakas and Fukuyamas get their affairs in order, including drawing up legal papers to transfer property from the male heads of households to their wives, because all local Japanese Americans had been alerted to prepare for evacuation from Juneau. President Franklin D. Roosevelt

Incarcerated Japanese-born (Issai) Alaska men, Lordsburg, NM, Dept. of Justice camp, 1942. Front row, far left, Shonosuke Tanaka. Third from left, Kiichi Akagi. Second row, fourth from right, is Hikohachi Fukuyama. Fourth row, far left, is Katsutaro Komatsubara. Directly below him in a white cap is T. Kato with Henry Mayeda next to him. Back row, third from right, is Sam Kito, Sr.

had issued Executive Order No. 9066 on February 19, 1942, specifying the removal of all those of Japanese descent – nearly two-thirds of them American citizens – from the West Coast. No date was given for when the forced removal would occur.

Mike E. Monagle attorney, ca. 1970. (Courtesy of Alison Browne)

Ham told Chaney the workers managed to keep the laundry open during the turmoil. However, when the Army arrived to build camps and defenses near the new airport, the Triangle Cleaners got the contract for cleaning military uniforms. Knowing they would soon be sent away, the Fukuyamas sold their washing equipment and rented their building to the cleaners. Sam and Ham stayed on and worked for the new owners. "They had Sam do the washing, and I worked the press machines. They needed our help," Ham said. At the City Café, Bill and John Tanaka, still in high school, took on the tasks of closing the restaurant and storing all the equipment in the Ba house, the little structure near their home. Alice said she didn't know the source of family income from December to April. She told Chaney, "My understanding was that my father's bank account was frozen, so I don't know exactly where the funds came from to keep our life going."

During the ongoing uncertainty, an order was issued on April 3 by the Alaska Defense Command. A *Daily Alaska Empire* article ran the details: "All Japanese of half-blood or better, including all males 16 years of age or more, whether American citizens or not, must report to their nearest army post pending evacuation from the Territory." This was to be done by April 20. The Western Defense Command would decide where the Japanese Americans would go after reaching the states. Each adult could take 1,000 pounds of baggage, and the government would pay the cost of transport.

Ham recalled that, unlike those Japanese Americans in Western states, who could take only what they could carry, those in Juneau were able to ship ahead what they wanted. "I had a box spring and innerspring mattress, so I had it crated," he told Chaney. "They also crated my skis, ski boots and poles." It was supposed that the number of items Ham sent might have had something to do with his former service with the local Alaska Guard.

The *Empire* article said orders exempted "Japanese women legally married to white men who are citizens or those married to natives. It applies to everyone of Japanese parentage of more than half blood." Children were allowed to accompany their parents or guardians "on a voluntary basis." The article concluded by saying, "There has been no announcement made as to when or how the Japanese will be moved to the south."

A Special Graduation

As a result of the executive order, John Tanaka, the senior class valedictorian, would not be able to remain in Juneau for his high school graduation. Consequently, his fellow students and teachers organized a special ceremony for him to be held in the Juneau High School gym. On the afternoon of April 15, the service opened with musical selections by the high school's band to a packed and somber audience. In what the *Daily Alaska Empire* said "might have served as an object lesson in tolerance," John was awarded his diploma five days before his 18th birthday. The graduation ended with cheers for John led by the high school's two yell leaders and the band's playing of "The Star Spangled Banner."

Ham was there. "It was very emotional," he told Chaney. "Tears were falling." Nadine Metcalfe Price, one of Walter's classmates, told her brother, Vern, that the community packed the gym paying tribute "not only to John but his entire family." Jane MacKinnon said her mother-in-law, Hazel MacKinnon, wife of Simpson, decided John should have a graduation party and held one for him in her home. Two days later, the high school newspaper reported that Bill Tanaka received a card from nine classmates with dollar bills inside expressing their heartfelt appreciation for Bill's years as their friend and schoolmate. The signed names included those of his good friends Bob Pasquan, Rod Nordling and Kenny Thibodeau.

Other preparations for leaving continued. Ham told Chaney that Pastor Hillerman came to Ham and Sam's apartment at the laundry where he said, "We studied the catechism." They were baptized on Good Friday, and afterward the congregation came forward to congratulate them. Restrictions were placed on all Japanese Americans for owning firearms, radios or cameras. Alice owned a Brownie box camera, a prized possession she had just received at Christmas, and when she learned of the restriction for owning one, she remembered thinking how unfair it seemed that her camera would be confiscated. "It was just a little camera," she said. She decided to give it to her friend Katherine (Bavard) Traeger. Katherine's father owned California Grocery on South Franklin, and the girls often walked to school together. Katherine remembers being very touched by Alice's gesture.

Shonosuke and George Messerschmidt were good business friends, and George's San Francisco Bakery delivered fresh bread daily to the café. The baker and cook annually exchanged gifts on their birthdays; George made Shonosuke a birthday cake, and Shonosuke brought George a bottle of "spirits." George's daughter, Roberta

John Tanaka receives his diploma from school board member Russell Hermann, left, & Superintendent A.B. Philips, right. Juneau High School gym, April 1942.

JOHN TANAKA GETS DIPLOMA TODAY AT JHS

Special Graduation Exercise Held for Honor Student at School

A graduation exercise was held in Juneau High School this afternoon. Only one student took part, but to the others it might have served as an object lesson in tolerance.

The student was John Tanaka, who, although he was born in Juneau and has attended school for 13 years with the same group of seniors with whom he had expected to be graduated next month, is a Japanese, and thus must be evacuated with others of his family and race by April 20.

April 20 will be John's eighteenth birthday.

But he isn't bitter about his birthday present. He says it is right and fair that he should go with the others, although he hates to leave the school chums who have been his closest friends for years.

Daily Alaska Empire, April 15, 1942.

Tanaka Presented Diploma at Unique Graduation April 15

At a unique commencement exercise held more than a month early, one of J High's outstanding seniors of the class of '42, John Tanaka, was presented his diploma by Mr. Russell R. Hermann, Secretary of the board of directors for the Juneau City Schools.

Opening with musical selections played by the High School Band, the program at which several special guests were present included introductory remarks by Supt. A. B. Phillips in which John's excellent scholastic and extra-curricular achievements were mentioned. In thirteen years of school work in the Juneau Schools John has but five "C" grades, all the rest being "A's" or "B's." That this high scholastic standard was not maintained at the cost of burying himself entirely in his books is proved by his participation in the activities of the Science Club, Photo Club, Math Club, Honor Society, and Quill and Scroll.

His work on the editorial staff of Publications for all four years has been of the best with a great sense of responsibility evident both in the first two years and as associate editor last year and editor during the current year.

Cheers for John led by the yell leaders, Adrienne Glass and Astrid Holm, and the playing of the Star Spangled Banner by the band closed the program.

The J-Bird, April 24, 1942.

(Messerschmidt) Spartz, remembers the day the Tanakas were leaving. They heard a knock at the door, and there stood Nobu Tanaka with her two daughters. This was quite an event for the family, as the Tanakas had never visited the Messerschmidt home before. But, Roberta said, "They came because they were leaving, and it was proper for them to come to call because they were business partners. We ate cookies I'd made, and Alice and I took turns to see how our mothers were doing, because Mrs. Tanaka couldn't speak English and my mother couldn't speak Japanese. It was a very impressionable event," she said.

George Messerschmidt, 1980.
(JDCM 81.01.015K)

The forced removal of the Japanese American community took place sometime near the end of April. On April 23, a *Daily Alaska Empire* article reported that the Japanese were being evacuated from Alaska and said they would be brought to an assembly center in Puyallup, Washington. The removal was shrouded in secrecy, and the article noted that the "time of arrival and the port of disembarkation has not been announced because of military necessity." However, Professor Claus-M. Naske, in a journal article for the University of Washington, placed the removal as April 25.

The rain that had been falling for a few days was abating with daytime temperatures in the 40s when Alice watched a strange, gray vessel sail into Gastineau Channel. She said, "I wondered if that was the ship that would take us away." The families had been instructed to be packed and ready, but no exact time was given. "It was dark when an Army truck came for us and took us from the end of Gastineau Avenue behind our house. We left the sheets on our beds and dishes in the cupboard as we had a very short notice," Alice said. To a person, Juneau's Japanese Americans left their homes silently, with dignity and without protest.

Conflicting and devastating emotions were prevalent. Nobu's daughter Mary Abo told *Juneau Empire* reporter Melissa Griffiths that Max Lewis had to escort his friend Sam Taguchi to the transport. "He probably had a rifle, but he had to take him, send him away. He felt very bad about that," she said. Marie Darlin, a classmate of Walter Fukuyama's, said of the event, "They were well liked and a part of the community. I think it was one of the saddest experiences we had in Juneau." Mary said John's classmate Don Rude visited her brother years later in a Spokane hospital where he was ill with cancer and told him that his class should have laid across the gangplank or organized a protest when John was taken to the ship. "But," Mary told Griffiths, "at the time, I think no one knows what to do in a situation when the law says you have to do this."

Another classmate, John Dapcevich, said Bill Tanaka was a good friend of his. "It was terrible," he said. "I didn't know the families were taken until I read about it in the newspaper. The Tanakas and Fukuyamas were very nice families and hard workers. They never had a chance to say goodbye." Roberta Spartz said, "We couldn't believe what was happening. They just yanked them out of school."

Bill Tanaka told Alice several years later that he recalled watching a young boy, Mac Nakamura, 16, going aboard the ship all alone with his bicycle. His father, Masaki Nakamura, had been taken earlier with the Japanese aliens. His mother was Tlingit, and like other Tlingits, she was forced to make a heart-wrenching choice of either being removed with the Japanese Americans or remaining in Alaska with her other children. Katie Hurley, who had gone to school with Ethel Fukuyama for 12 years, told Chaney that she and a group of friends recalled standing on the dock in the cold of that April evening waving good-bye to Ethel and to her church youth group friends Ham and Sam. It was hard for Katie and her friends to believe they would be put in prison. "That's what we were upset about," she told Chaney. The shock reverberated throughout the community. As Sam Kito, Jr., who was taken from Petersburg, would later tell Chaney, "All the Japanese people that I ever knew or met growing up were integrated into the larger community. They were a part of our school life and the town's life."

Sam Taguchi told Alaska Japanese historian Ron Inouye he thought the ship's name might be Saint Michel, but wasn't sure, and noted that the transport arrived at 4p.m. and left at 10p.m. Aboard the transport, families were separated, with men below decks and women and children above. Sam told Inouye that the men were guarded by friends serving in the National Guard. Because Ham had been in the guard (Ham had been honorably discharged in 1941 for a physical disability), they designated him as spokesman for the Japanese Americans onboard. The men were allowed on deck only twice a day for fresh air and some time with their families. "These guys in the military, I knew them, and they weren't antagonistic. They tried to make you comfortable," Ham said.

Alice said about 20 Japanese American and Tlingit families from towns along Southeast Alaska joined the boat. "It was comforting because we could commiserate about being in the same boat, so to speak," she mused. These included family members of Saburo "Sam" Kito, Sr. and Katsutaro "Slicker" Komatsubara from Petersburg, and Kiichi Akagi of Killisnoo near Angoon, Alaska, who would all live in Juneau after the war. Saburo Kito's pregnant wife, Amelia, boarded with her three children Sam, Jr., Barbara and John, all members of Petersburg's Tlingit Dog Salmon Clan, Leeneidi. Saburo had come from Osaka to Petersburg in the early 1900s where he married Amelia Okegawa, who was born of a Tlingit mother and

Amelia Okegawa Kito, 1930.

Forced removal sites of Alaska's Japanese Americans to the Puyallup Assembly Center (Camp Harmony) in Washington. Most were then transferred to the Minidoka Relocation Center in Idaho.

(Kevin Haney map,
National Park Service).

41

Japanese father. The couple worked for Kaylor Fisheries before the evacuation, and according to Inouye, Saburo, a cannery foreman, had just received a raise. Katsutaro Komatsubara had immigrated to the United States in 1918 and worked as a lumberjack in Washington before joining his family in Petersburg where he eventually owned a restaurant. There he married Tsuyo Oyama, who was evacuated with their three children: Rose, Nancy and Patricia.

William Akagi, 22, was the only one of his Killisnoo family to board the transport ship. His father, Kiichi "Henry" Akagi, had already been shipped out with other Alaskan Japanese immigrants. Kiichi had come to Killisnoo from Hiroshima in the early 1900s as part of a contingent sent to work at the whaling station there to ensure that products sent to Japan were produced properly. His first marriage to Nellie Nelson produced five children: Betty, William, Joseph, Connie and Frances, all members

Kiichi Akagi, 1942.

of the Angoon Beaver Clan, DeiSheeTaan. After Nellie's death, Kiichi married Frannie Walters with whom he had a daughter, Mary.

Of Kiichi's children, Joe Akagi had volunteered for the Army before World War II began and was still in active duty. Kiichi's grandson, Randy Wanamaker of the Sitka Killerwhale Clan, KaagWaanTaan, said Betty worked in a Vancouver, Washington, hospital and was not interned. Connie drowned in a fishing accident right before the war, and Frances was cared for by her Tlingit relatives. Frannie and her infant daughter Mary, members of the Angoon Dog Salmon Clan, Leeneidi, stayed in Alaska. Wanamaker said Kiichi never mentioned the family's incarceration when he wrote letters from his DOJ camp to his deployed son, Joe.

Voyages to Seattle normally took three days. Upon arrival, the Alaskans were transported to the Puyallup Fair Grounds, which had been hastily converted into a temporary "assembly center," one of several detention facilities on the West Coast and incongruously called Camp Harmony. White-washed horse stalls, used as hastily erected barracks with only cots for furniture, served as lodgings. The Alaskans were the first to arrive, get processed and be issued alien registration cards. When buses from Seattle reached the fairgrounds, Ham was reunited with his girlfriend and family members. Amelia Kito delivered Camp Harmony's first baby, Harry, on May 18 in a Tacoma, Washington, hospital and would return to the detention facility's crude environment with her newborn.

The Empty Chair Event

At home, the Juneau High School senior class planned their graduation to include leaving an empty chair for their departed valedictorian, John Tanaka. His friend and classmate Erling Oswald wrote about that day, "Apart from knowing that we were destined to serve in the military, the only thing that marred our graduation ceremonies was the absence of my good friend and our valedictorian, Johnny Tanaka," Erling wrote. "Though Johnny did not attend the graduation ceremonies, he was not forgotten. School superintendent, Mr. A. B. Phillips, kept an empty chair for Johnny and lauded his accomplishments and hard work during his school years. I have always admired Mr. Phillips for this."

John Dapcevich remembers the graduation ceremony well because his brother Bill, a friend of John's, was graduating that day. The feelings he experienced were probably best expressed by Walter's classmate Adrienne Glass Cooley who said, "I remember the time well—the feeling of unfairness we all felt." Years later the event still moved Harry Sperling from the class of 1943. He was on the publications staff and in the Quill and Scroll Honor Society with John. "I was so glad they did that," he said about the graduation. "I think everybody felt that way."

Underclassmen Al Shaw and Jack Pasquan remembered, too, and said the empty chair was painted black. Walter's classmate Marie Darlin said, "They had chairs for the graduates on a platform at the front of the gym with the empty chair sitting among the rest of the class (there were 39 graduates). I remember the horrible feeling I had of seeing an empty chair up there." As longtime Juneauite Mary Lou (Fagerson) Spartz explained to Chaney about the community's response, "There were no

Marie (Hanna) Darlin.
(1943 *Totem* yearbook)

Japanese left in Juneau. It was a moment when this community came together in an act of quiet disobedience for the injustice of the internment." Shaw said of the occasion, "It was Juneau's finest hour." Even so, the betrayal of Japanese American civil rights was shocking, harsh, swift and absolute.

JUNEAU DURING WWII
by Marie Darlin

By 1940, Juneau had a population of approximately 5,700, and all of us living here knew the U. S. was preparing for war. For Juneau this meant many of our residents had already relocated to Sitka to work on a military project, and our National Guard had been re-activated. After the Pearl Harbor attack on December 7th, we were told to cover our windows for the nightly blackouts ordered by the government for the entire Pacific Coast, and the community began to change. Our Japanese families were sent to internment camps in Washington and elsewhere. Families of federal employees left Juneau and traveled back to the lower 48, a trip that was very different then than it is today. Alaska was still a territory and not a state, therefore we were designated a foreign country by the military and travel permits were required to enter or leave Alaska.

Military forces for the war effort began arriving in Juneau in 1942. First to arrive were the 42nd Engineers from New Jersey who set up camp at Duck Creek. Later, the 137th Infantry came from Arkansas and Oklahoma and set up camp at Montana Creek Road where the community garden is now. Both camps were located in areas close to the airport and Mendenhall Glacier that, at the time, were considered very remote to the small population of Juneau, who mainly lived close to the downtown or in Douglas. The military set up a sentry post on the only road leading from the Mendenhall Valley to town near the Smith Dairy, which today is Valley Lumber on Old Dairy Road. The sentry post was a mandatory stop for anyone traveling to and from downtown and out the road. One would often find soldiers at the post who were heading to town and in need of a ride. Any place beyond that sentry point was considered a part of the military reservation. The military was also found in downtown Juneau. Femmer's Dock, located off of Willoughby Avenue where the Coast Guard dock is located today, became the subport – an embarkation port for military supplies headed to the westward ports of Seward and the Aleutians.

Juneau did their best to make the soldiers feel like a part of the community. We had a USO club and an Officers Club, and families always invited soldiers to dinner and other family activities. Dances were provided by the local service clubs and other organizations. Many of the Juneau men who enlisted were sent to the Seward and Aleutian areas because of their knowledge of boats and seamanship. Some served their basic training time at Montana Creek and were then sent north.

Businesses were faced with a much reduced schedule of steamship service bringing supplies and merchandise from the lower 48. If the weekly ship was delayed, grocery stores could run low on some items and would often trade items between themselves to keep the shelves stocked, but only tires were rationed in Alaska. The biggest change for the town was the 1944 closing of the Alaska Juneau Mine (AJ), located in downtown Juneau near where the tram is today. When the war began, it was considered a non-essential industry. Many of the miners joined the military or began working in the fishing industry. Except for a few Quonset huts and memories from those of us who were here at that time, there is not much left to remind us of the 4,000 to 5,000 troops who were stationed in Juneau during WWII.

MINIDOKA

In August 1942, the families held at Camp Harmony began boarding a train, its shades drawn, for a long ride. They were headed to Minidoka Relocation Center set in an isolated and arid section of Southwest Idaho. "I remember it as being hot and the old train had straight seats," Ethel Fukuyama told interviewer Hoshiko. "You couldn't sleep." Upon arrival at their new location, Alice's first memory of Minidoka was watching her feet slough through thick, dust-like sand. As she and her family soon discovered, Minidoka was no ordinary camp, but one surrounded by barbed wire and armed guard towers. Minidoka's Dakota Sioux name, meaning "a fountain or spring of water," stood in stark contrast to the locale's reality.

Minidoka encompassed more than 50-square miles with 36 housing blocks, 12 barracks in each block and six units per barrack to accommodate 10,000 people. Each block contained a laundry and bathroom building, a recreation hall and a mess hall. The site's other multi-use

Block Six incarcerees, Minidoka Relocation Center, 1942. The second little girl in front from the right is Mary Tanaka Abo standing in front of her mother, Nobu Tanaka. (Minidoka Interlude)

facilities included schools, places of worship, fire stations and a hospital. The Fukuyama, Komatsubara and Tanaka families were located in the same section called Block 6. The Kito family was in Block 24.

The Tanaka's new home, a 25 x 20-foot room for the family of five, was sparsely furnished with a pot-bellied stove, an Army cot with a straw mattress for each person and a single light socket hanging from the rafters for illumination. The room also lacked plumbing and cooking facilities. Water and coal for the stove had to be hand-carried from

Single light socket and bare ceiling in Minidoka barrack unit.

Wood planking of a Minidoka barrack.

central locations, and when fuel supplies ran low, they were supplemented by sagebrush gathered from the surrounding fields. Shrub and scraps of lumber left from the site's construction were soon recycled by incarcerees into makeshift furniture.

Drafty gaps between the wood slats of the barrack floor made it impossible to prevent the relentless sand and blinding dust storms from entering the room. Without insulation, trying to keep warm in frigid winter temperatures and cool in soaring summer heat was a continual challenge. In addition to the sparseness of the room was the total lack of privacy between the six units that comprised the barrack. Gaps extended from walls to open ceilings above the rooms, which allowed all sounds to be heard by neighboring families.

Reconstructed guard house, Minidoka Relocation Center.

The necessity of using communal latrines, devoid of partitions, further underscored the degrading reality of the families' incarceration. "The physical standards of life in the relocation centers have never been much above the bare subsistence level," the War Relocation Authority wrote in a 1943 report. "For the great majority of the evacuated people, the environment of the centers—despite all efforts to make them livable—remains subnormal and probably always will be." While the WRA report indicated that such centers as Minidoka were never intended for a long stay, or to be incarceration camps or places of confinement, that information clearly had not been conveyed to those forcefully removed from their homes. "They say the reason why they put us in there was for our protection," Saburo Kito later told

Claus-M. Naske, who wrote about the relocation of the Alaskans. "The only thing I can't figure out, guards were at the four corners. The guns were pointed at us all the time and not outside."

During their first days at Minidoka, Alice and her siblings were mainly concerned about Nobu. "My mother had always relied on my father who was the anchor in my family," Alice said in an interview conducted by California's San Leandro Library. "I think (the incarceration) left her in a real state of anxiety. When we got to Minidoka, we had breakfast every morning at the mess hall. She would collect the toast, bring it back to our room and dry it even more. She collected it in little boxes and put them under our cots." Alice continued, "We were all quite alarmed and worried that Mama was losing it. To us, it didn't seem like a sensible thing to do. I think we realized, too, she didn't think we were going to get food, so that showed the state of her mind. It was a relief when one day she realized this was a futile thing to do, and she gave up hoarding the toast."

Nobu Tanaka and daughter Mary in Minidoka, 1944.

Bill Tanaka, who was 14, later told his sister Mary that he had looked forward to a time when he would have more freedom from working every day at his dad's café and, consequently, viewed forced removal and incarceration as a kind of adventure. However, once he experienced the realities of Minidoka life, like scavenging for wood to make furniture for the family's barrack, he would later acknowledge the hardships. Observing the guard towers and barbwire surrounding the site made him realize he had actually lost his freedom. Bill also noted how the new living arrangements disrupted the family unit. He said, "You know, you really understand how a family group can deteriorate because in camp you could eat at any mess hall, so you weren't dependent upon your parents for food or shelter…. I could feel it myself because I didn't have to answer to anybody."

John and Alice sought ways to cope with incarceration, sometimes by corresponding with friends back home. In October, the Juneau High School newspaper, *The J Bird*, published an update about John saying that several students had received letters from him. "His camp is situated in the center of a large plain," the article said. "Upon completion the camp will be 2 ½ miles long and ½ a mile wide." In writing to his friend Skip, John expressed the desire to "trade some Juneau rain for some of the hot Idaho sunshine." Alice's second grade teacher, Mabel (Monson) Burford, wrote her encouraging letters, and she often heard from her friend Roberta (Messerschmidt) Spartz. "She answered my letters by writing on the back of mine because she didn't have paper of her own," Roberta said. She was very touched by the artwork Alice added to her letters, particularly her drawings of birds. Ironically, Roberta experienced her own wartime trauma. As a child of German descent, she said she was so taunted and bullied because of her heritage and the circumstance of Germany as a United States enemy, that she stopped speaking for quite some time.

The Tanaka's first Christmas in Minidoka was made a bit brighter with the arrival of presents from the John Hermle family. Mary unwrapped a doll, and in her package, Alice found a blue dress embroidered with delicate pink roses across the bodice. (See "The Blue Dress"

Minidoka Relocation Center 5th grade children, 1942. Alice Tanaka is third from right in front wearing the blue dress the John Hermle family sent her for Christmas.

story at the end of this chapter) She said of the gifts, "The Hermles extended such grace to us that first Christmas. It wasn't just about the presents. A more precious gift was their unspoken support."

The main focus for the Tanaka and Fukuyama families, as well as other incarcerated Japanese Americans, was to get their fathers transferred from the Lordsburg, New Mexico, Department of Justice prison camp and into Minidoka. Incarcerated lawyers and other supporters helped families write letters to the DOJ authorities. Attorney Mike Monagle did what he could from Juneau to reunite the families. In the effort, John Tanaka wrote a cover letter, also signed by Nobu, to General Simon D. Buckner at Fort Richardson in Anchorage, Alaska, on April 3, 1943. With the letter, John included affidavits written by several of the same prominent Juneau businessmen who had also written them for Shonosuke's Juneau hearing: M. E. Monagle, Dave B. Femmer, Roy

Rutherford, Cash Cole and J. F. Mullen. They testified at length about the incarcerated Shonosuke's allegiance to the United States and asked for his release. All swore to Shonosuke's loyalty and how he had contributed to charitable and community affairs without question or hesitation.

Mullen, president of B. M. Behrends Bank, wrote, "I have never heard him say anything, nor have I ever seen him do anything, nor have I heard of his doing or saying anything that would lead me to believe that he was not loyal to the United States. He was a hard worker, industrious, thrifty, honest, reliable and trustworthy." Rutherford, president and general manager of Juneau Lumber Mills, Inc., which was located next door to the City Café said, "The lumber mills has had accounts with him each year and we have always found him (Shonosuke) square, honest and fair in all his dealings. I have never heard his honesty questioned." John also wrote to the general regarding his father: "In the event you find that he is loyal and not dangerous we ask of you to grant him a rehearing as a step towards his release so he will be able to rejoin his family at the Minidoka Relocation Project."

Years later, Bill Ruddy, a Juneau attorney, remembered Monagle talking about the incarceration. "Mike Monagle was one of the nicest people you would ever want to meet," Ruddy said. But when he talked about the families' incarceration behind barbed wire, Ruddy said, "You could just see the rage boiling within him." Walter Fukuyama said Monagle took care of his family's legalities, finances and laundry building details while they were gone, including renting the laundry's upstairs rooms to the Army's United Service Organization members. Walter's daughter Nancy said, "The family often said that if it weren't for Mr. Monagle, the laundry building might have been lost to the family."

Juneau's Japanese American Incarcerees
1941-1951

Kiichi "Henry" Akagi

William Akagi

Hikohachi Fukuyama

Mume Fukuyama

Ethel Fukuyama

Walter Fukuyama

Thomas Fukuyama

Usuke Hamada

Hakuio Inouye

Thomas Itabashi

Shikanosuke Ito

Torao "Bob" Kanazawa

T. Kato

Utaka Kazama

Saburo "Sam" Kito, Sr.

Amelia Kito

Barbara Kito

Harry Kito

John Kito

Sam Kito

Katsutaro Komatsubara

Tsuyo Komatsubara

Rose Komatsurbara

Nancy Komatsubara

Patricia Komatsubara

Gary Komatsubara

Takashi Kono

Haruo "Ham" Kumasaka

Torihei Kuwamoto

Kojiro Matsubayashi

Henry Mayeda

Takao "Mack" Mori

Toyojiro Moriuchi

Thomas Mukai

Mark Nakamura

Masaki Nakamura

Paul Schimizu

Yakei Shiota

Takeshi "Gim" Taguchi

Isamu "Sam" Taguchi

George Tamaki

Shonosuke Tanaka

Nobu Tanaka

John Tanaka

William Tanaka

Alice Tanaka

Mary Tanaka

Saburo Tanaka

Toraichi Toyokawa

George Wada

Hiyo Yamamoto

Ikuichi Yoshida

Makato Yoshida

Correspondence between men at the Lordsburg Department of Justice camp and their families in Minidoka was sketchy at best. The families of Shonosuke Tanaka and Hikohachi Fukuyama received heavily censored letters. Alice said, "Sometimes something was either cut out or blacked out." The families had yet to know what transpired after the men were taken from Juneau in January of 1942. Still, they corresponded as best they could. While still separated from his father, in 1943 Walter wrote him this plaintive letter: "School is out in Juneau now. Only 34 students graduate this year. Just think, I would have been the 35th student if I were back home," he wrote. "I sure miss going skiing, hunting and fishing. Gee, remember we used to go blueberry picking, and make pies and jams with them. And used to go to Montana Creek and catch trout. Well after the war we can go back and do those things again. Gee but I wish you could be here with us." He also told his father that he had written to the Department of Justice in Washington, D.C., asking for his release from Lordsburg. Walter later saved the letters he had sent to Hikohachi. They were stamped, "Detained Alien Enemy Mail Examined."

Like many concerned about the circumstances of their relatives still living in Japan, the Fukuyamas worried about their daughter Mary's well-being, since she was still living and studying there. Ten months after her family's incarceration, Mary wrote a brief letter to her brother Walter from Tokyo. Thinking the Fukuyamas were still in Juneau, she addressed it to both their Juneau post office box and to the Juneau Laundry's street address. Her concern for them is palpable. "Mama, Poppa, are you well? I am worried. Are the Tanakas well, too? Are you altogether?" Mary wrote. "I am staying as a boarder and doing fine. I am studying. I am praying that you are well and I will see you again, Sumiko (Mary Fukuyama)."

A letter from Mary Fukuyama in Japan to her family in the United States.

Since mail delivery between the two countries had been officially terminated, Alice said that Mary Fukuyama's letter arriving at Minidoka was like a miracle. Apparently the delivery process had been shepherded through various channels by the American Red Cross.

Meanwhile, construction in Minidoka brought work to the Tanaka and Fukuyama teenagers. Walter told Chaney he had first worked with John Tanaka in the block's kitchen, but because the Alaskans were some of the first to arrive in Minidoka, they were offered construction positions. Walter and John hired on as linemen for the dangerous work of hanging from telephone poles while drilling holes and stringing wire. Later, as the nation suffered labor shortages because of the war, the WRA relaxed some of their rules, and the boys also worked with Bill Tanaka on a nearby Idaho truck farm. The National Park Service noted in a Minidoka site brochure that such workers were considered an "indispensable labor source for southern Idaho's agricultural-based economy."

In a letter to his father from a farm labor camp in Hazelton, Idaho, dated August 15, 1943, Walter explained his hours and wages: "This year I am working under contract which lasts till Nov. 15. I am to get 60 cents an hour. I work 10 hours every day. I am staying in a labor camp. I pay $1.00 (per) day for board. And I pay $1.00 a week for room. So far I been out here 2 ½ weeks. My gross profit so far is $104.00."

One of the teenagers' farm jobs, harvesting sugar beets, was considered crucial to the war effort because the vegetable's sugar was used for war munitions. Bill told Mary, "Pulling sugar beets is probably one of the most backbreaking jobs there is." He was referring to the short

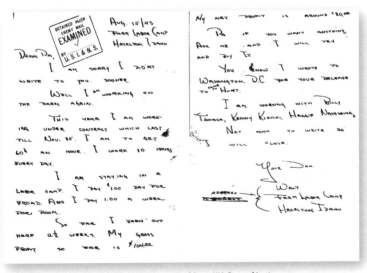

Walter Fukuyama's letter to his father, Hirohachi, in a Lordsburg, NM, Dept. of Justice camp.

hoe, which was later outlawed, used to dig the beets. He said a single row was over a mile long. They couldn't stand while working with such a short implement, but Bill said John was always 50 yards ahead of everyone else. "I don't know anybody that worked harder than my father, and I don't know anybody who worked harder than my brother," Bill said. Once some kids threw rocks at the workers while they were riding in the back of a farmer's truck, and Bill recalled thinking, "We could get killed and we wouldn't even make it in the newspaper."

As the WRA restrictions relaxed, other family members and friends also found work inside and outside of Minidoka. Walter's sister Ethel took an on-site clerical position, and his mother worked in the block's mess hall. Sam Taguchi, who, like Ham Kumasaka, was reunited with his Seattle family in Puyallup and Minidoka, first worked in the camp's laundry and then with his brothers, Susumu and Gim, on local farms picking sugar beets and potatoes.

The NPS brochure recounted the resourcefulness of those incarcerated despite their deplorable environment. "They built baseball diamonds and small parks with picnic areas. Their baseball team was virtually unbeatable. Taiko drumming and other musical groups were formed and a newspaper, the *Minidoka Irrigator*, was published. To create beauty in an otherwise dismal landscape, paths were lined with decorative stones and traditional Japanese gardens were planted." They also created vegetable gardens, a root cellar, a pig sty and a chicken farm.

The WRA, with approval from the Department of Justice in 1943, began allowing incarcerees to be sponsored for work or education in Midwest and Eastern states. Taking advantage of the opportunity, and after fulfilling the necessary requirements, such as having a definite destination and a means of support, Sam Taguchi left Minidoka for work at a Sidney, Nebraska, arsenal. From there, he moved to Rochester, Minnesota, working in the hospital where his sister Kimi was a nurse. A little later, he moved to Chicago and worked in a pinball factory. Bill Tanaka, now 17, relocated to Chicago, too, because he was told prejudice was less apparent there than other places. His first job was working for the American Brake Shoe Co.

That same year, like his friends Sam and Bill, Ham also headed for Chicago. On the way, he stopped at the Lordsburg DOJ camp to visit his father, whom he hadn't seen since 1941. "It was a very emotional thing," he told Chaney. Because he wasn't allowed to carry papers into the visiting room, Ham memorized everything he wanted to say, including the information his family had asked him to relay. The next day he was allowed to visit Shonosuke Tanaka and Hikohachi Fukuyama and conveyed memorized messages from their families as well. Lordsburg closed that year, and in June the men were transferred to a Santa Fe, New Mexico, camp.

Also during 1943, the 442nd U. S. Army Regimental Combat Team composed of Japanese Americans was formed. "There were some who felt that, on principle, they would not answer the draft call to serve in the military unless everyone in the camps were allowed to return home," Alice said. "There were others who volunteered to serve in the all-Japanese American combat force. They felt that by serving they would prove they were loyal Americans. Evidently, in some of the camps, this division was very strong and fights even erupted. I don't remember this about Minidoka. In fact, Minidoka had the highest number of volunteers of all the camps." She recalled a long discussion about this issue with friends 70 years later. "We all agreed that both sides had merit," Alice said. "They were all such young men, most in their late teens, and the situation of being in the camps was not an easy one."

Tooru Kanazawa was 36 and pursuing his writing career in New York City when he volunteered for the 442nd. He would serve in Italy and France, subsequently earning a Bronze Star. Joseph Akagi, Kiichi's son, had volunteered for the Army prior to World War II and was already serving with General Patton in North Africa in an elite shooter unit with the Third Infantry Division when the 442nd was formed. Joe's son Randy Wanamaker told Chaney that some Army officials came to Joe's unit and tried to make him transfer into the 442nd because of his ethnicity.

Joe Akagi, 1937.

Joe's commander became enraged after Joseph was told that if he signed a loyalty oath, he could stay where he was. Wanamaker said the commander "started yelling that they weren't going to ask one of his combat veterans from the front lines to sign a loyalty oath. If they wanted a loyalty oath signed, he was going to drag them up to the front lines under fire and (they could) get it up there where they might do some good." Joseph stayed with his division, which later liberated one of Germany's concentration camps. The experience haunted him, and Wanamaker told Chaney his father talked to Dr. Walter Soboleff, a Juneau minister, about it after the war. Soboleff later told Wanamaker, "Randy, I still get nightmares when I think of it. It was awful what your dad had seen." A bronze and silver star were among the many awards Akagi received for his service.

Alice said her brother John wanted to volunteer for the 442nd, but Nobu convinced him that she needed him in Minidoka until his father was back with the family. Shonosuke, desiring that reunion, considered the U. S. government's offer to incarcerated Japanese aliens of repatriation to Japan. He wrote to his family in Minidoka about this possibility, but his sons were strongly opposed, and he dismissed the idea. The Tanakas were finally reunited in March 1944. Nobu and the children were anxious to hear what had happened to Shonosuke after his forced removal from Juneau. Alice said, "I can still picture in my mind that lengthy conversation in our barrack room with all of us listening so intently to my father's telling of his experience."

Three Juneau Japanese men did not savor such reunions. Two had died in Department of Justice camps: Toraichi Toyokawa, the landscaper who assisted Nobu with her garden and raised a pet bear cub, and Torao Kanazawa, a waiter at the City Café for many years. Torao's brother, Tooru, told his family that he thought the prison environment had crushed his brother's spirit. In addition, Alice said that the memorable and dashing City Café waiter, Takashi Kono, was found to have entered the country illegally and had been sent back to Japan.

As the younger Japanese Americans moved out of Minidoka and into military service or East for employment opportunities, their fathers and other Japanese aliens continued to be reunited with their families. Now that Shonosuke was finally paroled to Minidoka, he took on the familiar work as a cook in the block mess hall, and John joined the 442nd. Nobu then followed the Japanese tradition of Senninburi. This required the sewing of 1,000 red knots onto a rectangular cloth, each knot added by a different woman. The cloth was to be worn in battle for protection. Fortunately, the war ended while John was on a troop ship headed for Europe, and the 442nd unit became part of the occupation force in Italy. One of his jobs was to guard over 200 German prisoners of war. Jeanne, John's future wife, told Chaney that John said he was shaking in his boots, saying they could easily have overtaken him. She said the prisoners were confused by John's ethnicity and wondered why he was on the other side of the war, not realizing he was a Japanese American.

Though Sam Taguchi could not serve because he had contracted hepatitis as a young man, his brothers, Susumu and Gim, were drafted. Gim, who would later come to Juneau to work with Sam at the City Cafe, served with the Military Intelligence Service as an interpreter during the American occu-

John Tanaka and family at Minidoka: L. to R. Alice, Nobu, John, and Shonosuke with Mary in front.

pation of Japan. He was an accomplished athlete, and after VJ Day, he played third base for the Fifth Air Force team, some of them former New York Yankee players, in good-will exhibition games with Navy and Japanese teams. At one point, Gim received an invitation to try out with the St. Louis Cardinals. "He was very talented and probably could have played professionally," family friend Kim Metcalf said, "but in those days you had to pay your own way to try out." Following his service, Gim joined Sam in Chicago where he played on Sam's basketball team, the Huskies, which did well against Japanese League teams along the West Coast of the United States.

After graduating with his high school class in Minidoka, Walter Fukuyama was also drafted, sent to Military Intelligence School and then to Japan with the occupation forces where he witnessed the war's devastation. He said everything in Tokyo was flattened. He saw homeless people living in tin huts and eating out of garbage bins. Naturally, Walter's main concern was whether his sister Mary was still alive. After contacting and talking with relatives, he found her, and they experienced a joyous reunion. Walter also met his future wife, Emiko Futori, while stationed there. After Hikohachi was reunited with his family in Minidoka, his daughter Ethel took her brother Tom to Washington, D. C., where she worked for the War Relocation Authority, and Tom finished his senior year of high school. Mary Fukuyama joined them there when she was free to return from Japan to the United States after the war.

When the war finally ended in August 1945, the Tanaka family was still in Minidoka awaiting permission from the Justice Department for Shonosuke to be discharged from parole. That September he appealed to the Enemy Alien Control Unit in the DOJ. "We naturally wish to return to our property where we can reestablish our home," he wrote. "I have no property or investments in Japan nor desire to return there." Shonosuke's parole was granted, and the Tanakas were finally going home.

Minidoka Internment Camp officially closed on October 28, 1945. By that time, according to the National Park Service, the incarcerated Japanese Americans, in addition to their many other contributions to making life more habitable in Minidoka, had cleared and cultivated 950 acres of inhospitable land and constructed all the ditches and canals needed to irrigate them. Walter Fukuyama's daughter Nancy said, "Despite their circumstances (at Minidoka) I don't remember ever hearing any bitterness from any of the Fukuyama family members."

THE BLUE DRESS
by Alice Tanaka Hikido

While rummaging through a box from the past that contained bits of memorabilia, I ran across a black and white photo taken in Minidoka Internment Camp, a desolate area of Idaho where we were sent during World War II. I picked the photo up to look at it more closely and found myself returning to that time and place some seventy years ago. There I was in the front row among other little fifth grade girls. As I scrutinized the picture, I realized that a photographer must have been given special permission, because cameras were not allowed in camp. The picture captured a sense of excitement. My normally straight hair held bouncy curls, and the girl's faces were graced with innocent smiles. I remembered wearing a very special light blue dress with a waistband of embroidered pink roses. The material was soft and graceful. Could it have been made of silk? As my memories came out of the shadows, I found myself going back to December 1942, that first Christmas in Minidoka.

I don't think I believed in Santa Claus at this point, but if I did, how would Santa ever find our barrack, let alone our singular room that barely had space for the five sleeping cots which were provided for my mother and the rest of our family? Decorations in the sparse barrack room that was now our home were non-existent, and the only Christmas tree was in the mess hall where we assembled each day for our meals. On top of all that, our father was still separated from us, detained in a different camp in Lordsburg, New Mexico. There was not a whole lot of joy to spread around. During this bleakness, I yearned for our home in Juneau and its simple, innocent rhythm of life. How quickly our lives were turned upside down in just one year.

About this time we got a notice that a package had arrived and was being held for us in the postal area. We were a bit astonished. Who would be sending us a package? My brother said he would go to get it, but we all wanted to go with him. We were that excited. We ran out of the barrack room, past the latrines, past the mess hall and arrived breathlessly at the postal office. The package was handed over and we could see that it had come from our hometown of Juneau, Alaska. It was from my father's friend, John Hermle. We just looked at each other in amazement and while taking in the thoughtfulness of Mr. Hermle, we quickly went back to the barrack and opened the package.

Among the items in the box were colorful Christmas candy, a beautiful doll with curly, blonde hair for my little sister, Mary, and a wonderful blue dress for me. As I remembered it, the blue was like the blue of Alaska's state flower, the forget-me-not, so light and pure. The delicately embroidered roses on the waistband of the dress made a statement of elegance. It was so pretty. I remember my mother hastily putting it back into the tissue wrappings as if to protect it from the rough, barren life of Minidoka. At the time I wondered if I would ever have a chance to wear it, but I was wrong about that. My mother must have remembered the dress when informed that a class picture was going to be taken. She sought it out from under our sleeping cot, and knew that I would have a ready smile to go with it. I'm grateful that the picture was taken so that many years later I could still be reminded of that Christmas.

Mr. Hermle extended such grace to us that first Christmas. It wasn't just about the presents. A more precious gift was his unspoken support during a time when we were treated like the enemy by our government. We were prisoners in a secluded internment camp far from home and denied our rights as Americans. There were other Christmases in Minidoka, but John Hermle's act of kindness made that first Christmas memorable, never to be forgotten. I tucked the photograph safely away back into the box of memorabilia. There will be a time when my memories will fade, but the gift of the blue dress sent by a thoughtful friend will always be captured and kept strong by this picture from the past.

HOME

When the Tanakas returned to Juneau in 1945, it was to a much quieter town. The noise of floatplane engine maintenance at the Alaska Coastal Airlines wharf and the roar of takeoffs in Gastineau Channel remained, but the gold mine had closed in 1944 because of skyrocketing costs during the war, and the relentless 24/7 bustle of the town had ceased. Unlike the experiences of other incarcerees who returned to hostile communities, the Tanakas were welcomed home. From the deck of their steamship that October evening, 12-year-old Alice recognized John Hermle and members of the Tanner family waving at them from the dock.

The Tanners, longtime friends who owned the Scandinavian Rooms near the City Cafe, invited the Tanakas to stay with them until they could return to their rented home. Some of the Tanakas' furnishings were damaged or missing; however, Alice said they found Emery Valentine's portrait still hanging on the living room wall. "It was one of the few things that remained when we returned," she said. "I think when our parents saw it hanging there, they took it as a good omen." Although Nobu found her garden suffering from neglect, Alice said she eventually concentrated on it again, slowly working away to reclaim its original beauty, her source of solace.

Illustration of Nobu's garden by Dale DeArmond, 1955.

Before the war, Shonosuke had leased the City Café building from Ole Orsen, whose grandson, Erling Oswald, was a friend of John's. However, by war's end Ole had died, and another restaurant was operating in the café's space. Regardless, Ole's family was very supportive, and Alice said they made it possible for Shonosuke to obtain the lease again. "The gesture was a very important factor in picking up our lives," she said. Other Juneau residents also lent support. "When our family started the café again, we had to borrow from the bank," Alice said. That's when Behrends Bank President J. F. Mullen personally guaranteed Shonosuke a loan, and his old friend George Messerschmidt of the San Francisco Bakery extended him credit for the café's daily bread orders.

Another friend, John Hermle of Home Grocery, saw an opportunity to repay Shonosuke. As a youth, Hermle delivered groceries to the café, and when he later decided to open his own grocery, Shonosuke encouraged him. In fact, Shonosuke and George Messerschmidt's father, Gus, who was also Hermle's uncle, co-signed a loan for him. Now Hermle told Shonosuke that he wouldn't have to pay his grocery bills until he had established a cash flow. The generosity of the men who gave him a hand when he returned to Juneau deeply touched Shonosuke. "My father was always very thankful about that," Alice said.

"I think that made him realize, too, that Alaska was really his home."

One regular customer, a Yugoslavian janitor, also never forgot Shonosuke's kindness. "Before the war sometimes people would be down on their luck, and they would come to my father for a small loan," Alice told Chaney. This was the case with the Yugoslavian. She said Shonosuke kept track of such transactions in a ledger. After he returned to Juneau, the Yugoslavian customer brought Shonosuke cash to pay his debt. Shonosuke protested, saying that his ledger books had been lost during the war, but the

Hermle dinner party, 1948: L. to R. Front row: Mary Tanaka, Jack Hermle. 2nd row: Alice Tanaka, Nobu Tanaka, Helen Hermle, Jean Hermle, Josie Hermle. Third row: Marcel Hermle, unknown, Shonosuke Tanaka and John Hermle. John extended Shonosuke credit at his Home Grocery after the war.

man said he remembered how much he owed and gave Shonosuke the money. "Actually, this was at a time when every dollar was very important," Alice said. "I think that little act of returning a loan validated the feeling that father had for his customers, that his customers who provided his livelihood were really solid people."

In 1946, Bill Tanaka, now 19, returned from Chicago to help his father reopen the café by setting up business accounts, ordering equipment and working as the day waiter while his father, now 64, served as the day cook. When the café opened in April, to everyone's relief, the customers returned. Bill told Mary, "The first three or four months we didn't pay for anything, and I know that we were seven or eight thousand dollars in debt right away. I told Papa that I would stay until we were even." When John's Army discharge came through a year later, he returned to help at the cafe so that Bill could return to Chicago. Alice told Chaney that years later, every once in a while her father would say, "You know, when I really needed Billy, he came back to help. I always am thankful for that." Bill told Mary that their father modeled a respectful attitude that he wanted to develop with his own children.

Two new faces joined the café staff from time to time as cooks: Henry Mayeda, the night cook, and Usuke Hamada. Usuke and Shonosuke had been friends from the early years. That first Thanksgiving shortly after returning home from Minidoka, Alice said her father cooked a turkey dinner to celebrate their homecoming and that Usuke was there. "Mr. Hamada was a very pleasant person, very even-keeled and good natured," she said. "There always seemed to be a mutual respect between Hamada-san and my father. They had a long, shared history." Another new face at the café belonged to T. Kato, also a cook,

T. Kato worked at City Café after the war, 1950.

and a favorite of young Mary's. "He was a very amiable man. I remember him living upstairs in one of Mama's rented rooms. He had a hot plate where he cooked his own food, which I liked to taste. To me he kind of looked like a walrus with his white hair and white moustache." Of a returning worker, Saburo Tanaka, Alice said, "My father respected him very much for his reliability and character. He was very helpful to my father as he (Saburo) resumed his role of waiting on tables and being a short order cook. He was very much liked by all the customers."

Saburo Tanaka, ca 1940s.

Home again, John Tanaka resumed his active life in Juneau. Vern Metcalfe later wrote in a tribute to him that John became Commander of Juneau's American Legion Post while Vern also held that position with the Veterans of Foreign Wars. The two collaborated in bringing the organizations closer together and became fast friends. After three years, with John's help, the City Café had become a successful business again. The loan was paid off, and John was able to consider pursuing his desire to attend college. After discussing this with his father, John contacted his brother, Bill, in Chicago, who had earlier told them that Sam Taguchi was interested in returning to Juneau. Shonosuke presently offered partnerships to Sam and also to Katsutaro Komatsubara, whom Alice said Shonosuke had met while they were incarcerated in Lordsburg, New Mexico. Alice told Chaney, "I think the idea was that the business needed a younger person who was solid in English because someone had to do the business part of the work. That was going to be Sam's responsibility." She said, "I also think my father knew that it was going to take two people to replace John." Metcalf wrote that John worked unbelievable hours to help re-establish the café.

To assist in the transition, Bill Tanaka returned to Juneau, allowing John to begin attending the University of Washington in Seattle, which he funded through the G. I. Bill, working summer months at the café and managing a student house at college. Alice said that Bill stayed for a number of months until Sam and Katsutaro were comfortable in their new positions as co-partners and the transition was completed. When Shonosuke's health declined, she said Sam began managing the business details and serving as the day waiter, and Katsutaro, familiarly called Slicker, became the day cook. Fortunately, the partnership worked, and the café successfully continued serving hearty workmen's fare while also drawing newer and younger customers from other segments of the city. After Sam joined the cafe in 1949, he asked his brother, Gim, called "Jim" by the locals, to move to Juneau and work as the night waiter.

Meanwhile, John's sisters were adapting to being back in Juneau. Alice, now an adolescent, wondered how she would fit in after her long absence. She said, "I can remember feeling so alone and missing my old comfortable friends I had made in camp. In Juneau, old friends I had left behind in the fourth grade now seemed like strangers. I was keenly aware that my home on lower South Franklin Street, which was also populated by saloons and the red light district then, was definitely on the wrong side of the tracks. It was not an area I would feel comfortable inviting friends. However, I had to overcome my introversion to re-establish friendships."

The high school's Girls Athletic Association, where she enjoyed playing sports, helped Alice feel included. "Neither race, ethnicity nor status made a difference," she said. Though incarceration clearly shaped Alice's life, it was a subject she never shared with high school friends. "Perhaps I still retained a feeling of pain for being Japanese and wanted that chapter of my life to remain closed. At that time, all I wanted was to be a normal all-American girl concentrating on my studies and blending in with my classmates," she said. "By then I was working at the café after school and on weekends as a waitress where I knew I was making an important contribution to the family's effort to get back on its feet." She said after a few years her family was pleased to see the City Café again take its place in the Juneau community. "We were able to put the war years behind us."

On her return to Juneau, Mary was just starting kindergarten. As a toddler during her incarceration, she was used to seeing primarily the black hair and brown eyes of the Japanese Americans living there. Consequently, she was surprised when she noticed a girl with blue eyes and blonde hair in her class. She thought maybe her eye color was changeable, too. Lively and curious, Mary said she essentially grew up as an only child from age nine because her siblings moved away to college and careers.

After the war, Nobu and Shonosuke regained contact with their families in postwar Japan and learned of the hardships they were experiencing. Mary sometimes helped her mother fill out custom slips for the care packages Nobu mailed to Japan. "She bought warm clothes from the Salvation Army store and packed them with gum, candy and cigarettes," Mary said. "For each box, she called out the item's quantity and value for me to enter on the customs slip. I had a hard time adding up the estimates. Since I was only about nine years old, my figures didn't fit neatly into columns, and I had to do a lot of rechecking and erasing. Then Mama packed each box tightly with butcher paper and string before taking a taxi to the post office."

Nobu was happy to communicate with her family again and wrote many letters to make up for the lost war years, using her upstairs room in the café to write. "She was surrounded by Roi Tan cigar boxes of letters she received from them, and she wrote them many letters,"

The Tanakas: Alice, Nobu, John, Shonosuke & Mary, 1954.

Mary said. "I would often catch her just staring out into space." Nobu often added money orders to her letters, but didn't spend money on unnecessary things for her own family, saying money didn't grow on trees. Mary said her parents' reasoning indicated how they "wanted their children to have a better and easier life than theirs, and so they saved all their earnings for us."

Reflecting on her early years in Juneau, Mary told Chaney, "It took a long time not to be ashamed of being Japanese because of the war." She carried a strong memory of this feeling. Her mother, who never ventured far from home or the café, wanted Mary, then ten years old, to take her to the movie *Go for Broke* about the bravery of the 442nd Infantry Regiment during World War II. This was an unusual request because, Mary said, Nobu had never gone to a movie theater before. During the film, Mary thought the Japanese soldiers portrayed looked fierce and menacing, not realizing there was a difference between the Japanese Imperial Army and Japanese Americans in the 442nd fighting for the United States. Consequently, after the movie while walking home, Mary felt shame and didn't want to be seen with her mother, who she thought looked very foreign with her hair pulled back into a bun and dressed in an overly long dress. So she left Nobu and crossed the street. Mary said her mother must have sensed how she felt and never scolded her about the incident. "I lost pride in my ancestry for being seen as the enemy during World War II," Mary said about that time. "Regaining it was a long journey for me. Now I am proud of my Japanese heritage and of my American nationality."

Mary soon immersed herself in Juneau activities like Brownies, Girl Scouts and piano lessons. Later, she played piano at Rainbow Girls events and joined the Lutheran Church choir and its youth group. In high school she shot .22s at rifle club, sang in the chorus and marched with the pep club's drill team. She also used her interest in art by making posters for activities and decorations for school dances. At one point, she was encouraged to enter the annual conservation poster contest sponsored by the American Legion. She won the competition, which she said greatly boosted her self-esteem. The art teacher who helped her was Max Lewis, Ham and Sam's friend, who had returned to Juneau after the war.

"Luckily I had friends throughout my Juneau years who saved me from feeling too different," Mary said. "I was invited into their homes, and I saw how their lives were so different from mine. We didn't eat our meals together like other families I visited, because my parents were usually busy cooking or washing dishes, while I ate alone in a booth. They worked every day, all day and never took a vacation." Instead of eating family style, Mary was served from the cooking station with foods like halibut cheeks, boiled tongue with horse radish and roast pork or beef with mashed potatoes.

Mary also noticed a difference in how other families communicated. Her friends conversed easily in English with their parents, but, Mary said, "I didn't understand when my parents spoke Japanese to each other, since they spoke broken English to me. Somehow, I decided Japanese was their language and English was my language." Despite such differences between her life and those of her friends, the restaurant, where her father was the boss and where everything was familiar, made her feel

(Cont'd on page 87)

MY INDOMITABLE FRIEND
by Marjorie Shackelford

Author's Note: The City Café had been in existence for 35 years before the Tanakas were evacuated. When I met Mary Tanaka in third grade, her family had been in Juneau for two years following their Minidoka internment and were busy rebuilding their lives. While we were growing up, neither Mary, nor her parents, ever spoke to me about the humiliation of being interned. I found out about it quite by accident after college, but conversations of any depth took thirty years to develop, which shows just how indomitable Mary and her family really were.

I met my indomitable friend, Mary Tanaka, when I was eight years old in Miss Murphy's third grade class. However, where I really have her cemented in my memory is Junior Choir practice at the Resurrection Lutheran Church. We were altos, so we sat together during Sunday services, sang as one voice during church and giggled or whispered together during practice. One of the factors that motivated us to attend practice, without fail, was getting to wear sparkly tinsel crowns on our heads during the midnight service on Christmas Eve. From that early time spent together, a friendship grew.

The year was 1948 and I'd never really had a best friend yet, except for my sister Karleen, but that was the year Mary was to capture my undivided attention. She was very lively and chock full of ideas. Plans on how to spend our free time just flowed out of her. She was not a force to be denied as she possessed strong opinions, especially about how to treat other people. She seemed to know everyone no matter where we wandered, and she never failed to treat each person with positive attention and respect, even the scariest looking person on the street.

Juneau was only about five thousand people in those days, and I was allowed to go downtown on errands or to the movies during the day at a fairly young age. Mary was often my companion, but I didn't feel as eager to engage everyone in conversation as she did. Some of the people she knew were just too far out of my comfort zone. I'd hang back while she teased and laughed with a scruffy fisherman fresh off his boat or someone in a fancy suit from the Federal Building. But, frankly, she was so much fun and full of adventure that life was much more exciting when she was around. So, I swallowed my fears and obediently followed where she led.

The act that really forged our friendship was when she invited me to the City Café for lunch after church services. I was quite excited because I had never had the opportunity to go to a restaurant yet in my young life. My parents graciously gave their permission, and Mary and I walked down to the café together after services were over. As we flitted down South Franklin toward the docks and the Cold Storage, Mary again seemed to know many of the people we passed on the street. She greeted them all with enthusiasm and they, in turn, reflected her good will. Most of the

Mary and Margie in 3rd grade.

time, I simply said hello and managed to squeeze out a smile or two.

When we entered the café I began to feel a little shy. It seemed like everyone at the lunch counter turned around, looked at us and smiled at Mary. They all knew her. The fishermen, drinking their coffee with their white workmen's caps askew, greeted her with comments like, "Who's your little friend?" and "You gonna finally have some help behind the counter?" Mary just laughed and ignored them as she sauntered into the kitchen with me by her side, feeling as comfortable in her surroundings as I felt like a foreigner. It began to dawn on me how she knew so many different people.

This was a totally strange place to me, full of competing sights, smells and emotions. I was excited at the newness of everything while being a little nervous at all the attention we had been receiving. The two Japanese cooks were frantically busy chopping, stirring and yelling out their orders in a language I didn't quite understand. They wore white aprons smudged with various foods they had cooked that day. Short white circular hats like I'd seen in black and white pictures of restaurants in my mother's magazines were perched on their heads. They seemed too busy to even notice our presence. It was a little like being in another country for someone like me, having lived in Juneau all of my life and never having experienced exotic locales.

I followed Mary through the kitchen and into a back hallway lined with white wooden booths. The backs were so high, you couldn't see over them. They were built with narrow pieces of lath and covered in white shiny enamel paint. Each booth looked like a solitary and private hideaway. She motioned for us to sit in one. I felt encased in a little world all our own. It seemed quite grand.

About the time I had adjusted to my surroundings, Mr. Tanaka arrived with a gigantic smile on his face. Above all, I remember that smile. He was one of the cooks I had seen working in the kitchen. He seemed so delighted to see me that my discomfort faded away. I was a visiting dignitary, a welcome guest, an honored friend in a brand new world. He bowed his head slightly to me as Mary introduced us and said he was happy to meet me. He and Mary talked in a mixture of English and Japanese that I felt I should be able to interpret but couldn't quite grasp. It sounded like it was something about what to serve us for lunch. Then, as quickly as he appeared, he left.

Mary and I chatted awhile. I could hear slight background noises and she told me that people rented apartments upstairs. About this time a lovely Japanese lady with long skirts and a very quiet manner arrived. She smiled slowly at me as she placed silverware and napkins on our booth table. Mary introduced this lady as her mother and she too lowered her eyes and slightly bowed her head in greeting. She and Mary engaged in some animated conversation that also consisted of words in both English and Japanese. Then, with a soft smile, as quietly as she arrived, she departed.

Mr. Tanaka reappeared with two heavy oval white porcelain dishes balanced confidently on one arm. He placed one in front of me. What was sitting on the plate is very firmly set in my memory. Thick slices of turkey covered a giblet dressing nestled next to a helping of mashed potatoes topped in the center with a puddle of gravy. A pile of small canned peas (I didn't know about any other kind) and some jellied cranberry sauce added color to the dish. A crispy roll also graced my meal. Everything looked very tasty. I was eager to dig into my lunch, but I waited for some signal from Mary. She took a bite of her turkey, then I took one.

Her father beamed down at us. I took another bite, this time of the dressing, and told him how delicious it was. Mr. Tanaka continued to smile and disappeared again. As it turned out, it was all delicious. To crown the meal, he soon arrived with two slices of apple pie. I was pretty full, but I managed to eat every crumb of it. After all, I didn't want to disappoint him. It seemed very important that I enjoy everything he placed in front of me.

When it was time to leave, I thanked Mr. Tanaka and Mary profusely. I looked for Mrs. Tanaka, but she had disappeared somewhere in the building and I didn't have enough confidence to poke around and look for her. Mary escorted me to the front door of the café where I smiled gratefully at the cooks and customers and then walked up Franklin Street to my home on Fifth and Gold and excitedly told my family all about my special lunch at the City Café.

Food seems to dominate these early memories of friendship. When going to the movies, Mr. Tanaka would send a brown paper bag stained with oil and stuffed with tempura for Mary and me to munch on during the show, which we did with gusto. At Christmas there was a special sushi

Mrs. Tanaka made that, at first view, I wasn't sure I wanted to try. It took me awhile to appreciate the pungent taste of the seaweed covering the sushi, but I grew to love it. In high school, I tossed my tiresome baloney sandwich into the garbage when I saw that Mary had brought a lunch assembled at the café to share. It contained sandwiches filled with big slabs of roast beef, mandarin oranges and some crunchy and hot orange crackers.

Not to be outdone, I eventually took her to my grandma Alstead's house on Starr Hill where she secretly left her lunch in its paper sack leaning up against the back door so she could feast on Norwegian coffee cake and lefsa in my grandma's warm inviting kitchen. At our house, my mother baked a pie once while Mary was visiting and put sugar and cinnamon on the remnants of dough which she baked in the oven and gave to us to devour, and we did. Another time she stayed overnight and while cooking breakfast, my father showed her how he added water to the fried eggs and covered them so you didn't have to turn them over to firm up the whites. I had never noticed his strategy with the eggs before, but Mary was mesmerized and my father smiled at her enthusiasm.

Over time, I discovered the mysterious Buddha on the windowsill at the Tanaka's home, her mother's meticulously designed rock garden with its Japanese influence around their house and how to say thank you in Japanese. She in turn improved her sewing skills with my mother's guidance, enjoyed the strange accents, tastes and sights at my grandparents' home and learned how to say thank you in Norwegian.

It turns out that we didn't have to leave Juneau to learn about and enjoy other cultures. Our families quietly existed side by side in that small Alaskan town. They shared many similar beliefs. Both believed in the value of hard work and the dignity of the individual and conversely frowned on any behavior that smacked of bragging or self-pity. Each patriarch had come to Alaska from another country to make a new life for their family. They were willing to make the sacrifices and take the risks that move demanded of them.

With the innocence of young children, we delighted in discovering the varied details of each of these unique worlds and found them fascinating. I think the key to that exploration lay in both of our families' warm acceptance of each of us with no seeming reservations. And sometimes, when Mary and I are involved in a new adventure that feels a little risky, I like to think that they are looking down on us still and smiling.

comfortable and secure. Of course, all the while she was attending school, making lifelong friends and enjoying her activities, Mary continued working on Saturdays at the café until her junior year, when she began acquiring lucrative summer office jobs with the territory.

Meanwhile, the Komatsubaras also were adapting to the Juneau landscape. The family, which had expanded with two more children, Gary and Karen, settled into the apartment of the Tanaka home. Mary said Katsutaro was responsible for introducing flash-frozen Petersburg shrimp, which became a popular new entrée, and for the café's closing on Sundays, which became the Komatsubaras' family day. She said Katsutaro enjoyed joking with customers and knew their favorite foods. Longtime

L. to R. Katsutaro & Tsuyo Komatsubara, Nobu Tanaka by the City Café, 1955.

Juneau Senator Bill Ray remembered Katsutaro and his thoughtfulness. "When I came down to the City Café at 1 a.m. before I went fishing, Slicker always saved me something to eat from the previous day's dinner." Mary said of Katsutaro's wife, Tsuyo, or Rose, as she was called, "Mrs. Komatsubara's homemade cakes were a big favorite with customers."

Laws that denied citizenship to Japanese immigrants were finally repealed, and in 1956, Shonosuke and Nobu Tanaka became naturalized United States citizens. Also that year, John Tanaka married Jeanne Aoyama in Seattle. Jeanne, from Kent, Washington, had been incarcerated at Tule Lake Internment Camp in California and had recently returned to the United States after five years in Japan. She met John through a girlfriend in Seattle where John was attending the University of Washington and living at the Synkoa House for Nisei (second generation Japanese) students. Jeanne said she and John dated for two years until John was accepted by St. Louis University Medical School in Missouri. Before he was to leave, the couple had what Jeanne thought was one last date, a ferry ride to Victoria, British Columbia. On the way back, John proposed. After his first year at St. Louis, they married, and John worked as a lab technician while finishing medical school.

John's daughter Cathy told Chaney that a childhood medical emergency inspired her father to become a doctor. When John was 11, he had an operation for a ruptured appendix. "My dad said the doctor was pretty new at medicine, but he decided to keep his (John's) abdomen open to let it drain. This helped get rid of the pus and the infection, plus he was on antibiotics," Cathy said. At that time many people died from intestinal infections, so John felt the doctor had

Dr. John Tanaka with his children: L. to R Rich, Cathy, Dave. Liz is in John's arms, ca. 1960s.

saved his life. "My dad decided he wanted to be a doctor, too, so he could help others," Cathy said. "I became a nurse partly because of hearing that story from Dad." Mary also remembers hearing about John's hospital experience. John told her, "Papa stayed by my bedside, and the window was kept open to the winter air to keep my fever down."

John returned to Juneau less frequently, but stayed in touch with Juneau friends like Vern Harris, a fellow American Legionnaire, throughout his life. Vern's son

Dennis said Dr. Tanaka came for dinner twice when he was in town. "The first time my parents were hosting," he said, "and the second time he would bring Chinese food from the City Café, a big treat for us, since we didn't eat out very often."

Like John, Alice Tanaka also married in 1956 after meeting 442nd veteran Katsumi "Kats" Hikido in San Jose, California. Nobu and Shonosuke were able to travel to John and Alice's weddings, though Shonosuke had slowed considerably and was no longer able to work. Mary said his feet were so swollen with edema, he could hardly walk from room to room. When Shonosuke died in February 1957, his children returned for his funeral services. His old friends Hikohachi Fukuyama and Usake Humada were there, too. Mary, who was a high school junior then, said, "It was a cold, snowy, windy February day, and cars were lined up from the top of the cemetery hill to the bottom near the caretaker's shed where my father is buried. I remember feeling proud that he was well respected."

Alice spoke to Chaney about some reflective moments she shared with her father before he died. She asked Shonosuke why he had never returned to Japan. "In Japan there were a lot of social classes and sometimes you had to bow down to someone you really didn't respect," he told Alice. "But here in Alaska if you didn't respect somebody, you never had to bow down to that person." She also asked him how he felt about being in-

John Tanaka, M.D.

carcerated, losing his life savings and having to start all over again. Shonosuke told her, "You have to remember that nobody in our family lost their lives. In the war there were many people in Japan and America who were not that fortunate. We all came back. John came back. You know, we were very fortunate. It was hard times, but we were fortunate."

After Shonosuke's death, the café ably carried on with Katsutaro and Sam. Gim and Sam continued their interest in sports by sponsoring bowling and city basketball teams. Again, Sam coached while Gim played as a standout guard. Gim would later be inducted into the Juneau Lions Club Gold Medal Basketball Hall of Fame. Sam's devotion to sports was acknowledged in the 1960s when Governor Bill Egan, a frequent City Café customer, named him honorary Commissioner of Athletics for Alaska.

Over time, Sam became well known for his wry wit and irascible nature as he bustled about the café with a cigarette hanging from his lip, sharing opinions on issues of the day, usually concerning politics or sports, while simultaneously pouring coffee, taking orders and running the cash register. Customers and friends remember Sam well. Kim Metcalfe said, "Sam was a Republican and always hated Roosevelt, of course, for what he did (ordering the Japanese Americans to incarceration camps)." Former Juneau Senator Bill Ray said he was sitting at the counter once when a tourist off a ship came into the café. "And Sam, you know, with that cigarette hanging out of his mouth, walked over to the table," Ray said. "The tourist asked if they had any Chinese tea. Sam said, 'Yeah, we serve it all the time. It's called Liptohn.' I about fell off the stool." Roger Grummett spent time at the café where his basketball coach, Bill Ordway, often brought the Juneau High School team. "If Sam insulted you, you knew he liked you," Roger said. "When I was older, I went to the café early one morning, not my usual time, and sat at

Gim Taguchi, 1954

the counter. The café was pretty empty, but Sam told me I couldn't sit there. 'That's Kinky Bayer's chair,'" he said, referring to the café regular. "That was classic Taguchi."

Customers all knew stories about what happened if someone criticized Sam's food. One received a maple bar delivered upside-down on his plate. But the loyal customers also knew the good heart beneath the crusty exterior, and Sam had the patrons to prove it. As his sister Reiko Sumada tells it, "I understand he didn't charge some of his patrons at the café when they were unable to pay. That didn't surprise me." Eventually the City Café location was sold to the state for an Alaska Marine Highway ferry terminal site, so in 1964 the business moved across the street to 439 S. Franklin Street.

About that time, Mary said John made a trip to Juneau with his sons because he wanted them to see his home town. His son Ed told Chaney, "He took us to all his old fishing places, the City Café, the Russian Orthodox Church, all the stairs he used to climb to his house. But every block we would have to stop because he would know somebody, so it took us forever to see anything. But it was amazing that after that much time he still knew so many people, and everyone was so nice. I know he really missed Juneau."

In 1967, Nobu Tanaka died. Alice said of her, "I have come to appreciate the strength that she had. In the mid-1930s, a major landslide came down Mt. Roberts very near our home and took a number of lives. She was always mindful of the danger for a potential landslide as we continued to live in our home. Then a few years later, my brother Teddy disappeared and was presumed to have drowned off the city docks. Her security was again tested when World War II resulted in her forced evacuation from Juneau. I am totally in awe of how she was able to persevere in these circumstances."

Six years later when Katsutaro died, the Alaska State Senate passed Resolution 35 honoring him. It declared:

"Slicker was one of those Americans who suffered the indignation of being incarcerated in a relocation center during World War II and yet never lost his faith in America and in his adopted Alaska." The resolution went on to state that all who knew him would "miss this rare human being who possessed an indomitable wit" and who contributed "to the betterment of Juneau."

Sam operated the café until his retirement in 1982. Then, with his brother Gim, the two opened Taguchi's Fine Chow, which they ran for several years. In keeping with the Tanaka tradition, the restaurant served a wide cross-section of locals and visitors. "Sam and his brother Gim were the glue that held the café together," *Juneau Empire* reporter Jeanine Pohl wrote. "Gim cooked and Sam was the talk-show host. They fed some people for free, and most patrons had an account there. The Taguchi brothers never got rich off the City Café." When Sam died in 1995, Governor Tony Knowles ordered state flags to be flown at half-staff. Gim passed away two years later.

John Tanaka succumbed to cancer in 1977. He was 53. He had never told his children about the empty chair event and the graduation he missed. "John Tanaka was one of the finest human beings it has ever been my pleasure to know," Vern Metcalfe wrote. "He passed this way and Juneau was a better town for it." Before John died, on February 19, 1976, President Gerald Ford announced Proclamation 4417, which recognized Executive Order 9066 as a "national mistake" and acknowledged its "termination upon the issuance of Proclamation 2714, which formally proclaimed the cessation of hostilities of World War II on December 31, 1946." Proclamation 4417 was made as an "American Promise -- that we have learned from the tragedy of that long-ago experience forever to treasure liberty and justice for each individual American, and resolve that this kind of action shall never again be repeated."

Then in 1982, the Commission on Wartime Relocation and Internment of Civilians reported that Japanese

Americans and permanent resident aliens had been the victims of "race prejudice, war hysteria and a failure of political leadership." The commission declared that those incarcerated were denied their rights as American citizens *"despite the fact that not a single documented act of espionage, sabotage or fifth column activity was committed by an American citizen of Japanese ancestry or by a resident Japanese alien on the West Coast."* (Author's emphasis)

Sam & Gim shortly before retirement. (Mark Kelley, Juneau Empire)

In 1988, Congress passed the Civil Liberties Act which gave each surviving incarceree, around 60,000 people, reparations of $20,000 each. A letter of apology from President George H. Bush followed in 1990. Although parents of the Juneau families, the Issei, did not live to see the Civil Liberties Act signed by President Reagan in 1988, their children, the Nisei, who had also been incarcerated, received reparations and a presidential letter of apology. Mary Abo said she was grateful, and the long-awaited validation holds particular meaning for her. "I learned from these governmental acts that there is justice if it is persistently pursued," she said. "That's a history lesson worth passing on." Her sister, Alice, concurred and added, "It makes me proud that our nation can recognize and apologize for mistakes made. It's a humility that makes our country great." Still, she knows the empty chair story is a cautionary tale. Reflecting on the prejudice and war hysteria that sent 120,000 Japanese Americans to incarceration camps during World War II she said, "Fear is our enemy in uncertain times. We can't let fear grab us. We have to continually be vigilant, educated and informed so that what happened to us, never happens again."

THE WHITE HOUSE
WASHINGTON

A monetary sum and words alone cannot restore lost years or erase painful memories; neither can they fully convey our Nation's resolve to rectify injustice and to uphold the rights of individuals. We can never fully right the wrongs of the past. But we can take a clear stand for justice and recognize that serious injustices were done to Japanese Americans during World War II.

In enacting a law calling for restitution and offering a sincere apology, your fellow Americans have, in a very real sense, renewed their traditional commitment to the ideals of freedom, equality, and justice. You and your family have our best wishes for the future.

Sincerely,

GEORGE BUSH
PRESIDENT OF THE UNITED STATES

OCTOBER 1990

Letter of Apology from President George Bush, 1990.

Epilogue

Saburo Tanaka, waiter and cook at the City Café, worked for several years, carefully saving his wages. He then returned to Tokyo, Japan, to be with his parents. He eventually married and purchased a small apartment building he named the Juno Apartments in memory of his former home.

After the war, Tooru Kanazawa returned to New York where he married Masako Fuji in 1948 and raised two daughters and a son. During the early years of their marriage, Tooru served as the English language editor for the *Hokubei Shimpo*, later the *Nichibei*. To support his growing family, he worked as a travel agent for the New York Travel Service where he became vice president and retired in 1987 at the age of 80. Two years later his book *Sushi and Sourdough* was published. He continued to write until the end of his life.

Sam Taguchi died in 1995. His sister Kimi wrote in his memorial service program that Sam enjoyed the politicians of Alaska and their interest in matters of redress for the Japanese Americans incarcerated during World War II. "Several articles appeared of his testimonies," she wrote. Sam developed throat cancer and went to Minneapolis to be near Kimi during surgery and therapy. "But as soon as he could, he wanted to go home to Juneau," she wrote. "This affliction showed us, his family, as we gathered (in Juneau) how much everyone cared and why he wanted to live and die in Juneau. We are grateful to you all for the years of friendship and love you bestowed on our brother Sam." He was survived by his wife, Helen, and two daughters. His brother Gim married Janet Cooke in 1962 with whom he had two children and four stepchildren. In 1997, he died in Juneau of cancer at age 73.

After his move from Minidoka to Chicago, Ham Kumasaka married his Seattle girlfriend, Minnie Ota, a pharmacist. Referring to their forced removal and incarceration, Ham told Chaney, "My wife says, 'We are not going to look back. We are going to look forward,' which we did." Ham worked 50 years for Noma International, a Chicago Christmas light company, eventually becoming vice president. After retirement, Ham and Minnie returned to Seattle where they lived for the rest of their lives.

Sisters Mary Tanaka Abo, left, and Alice Tanaka Hikido visit Ham Kumasaka, age 94, 2013. Ham was among the first members of Alaska National Guard's Company A.

After his discharge from the service, Joe Akagi married Eunice Wanamaker, studied diesel mechanics on the GI Bill and then traveled Alaska repairing cannery equipment. He and his family lived in Juneau from time to time, as did his father, Kiichi, who ultimately preferred making his home in Killisnoo. Joe's son Randy Wanamaker, a geologist and former City and Borough of Juneau assemblyman, serves as vice chairman of Goldbelt, Inc., one of Juneau's Alaska Native corporations.

After his family's release from Minidoka, Saburo "Sam" Kito, Sr. worked at the Anderson Dam nearby. He then moved with his family to Juneau in 1946 where his wife worked at the City Café, and he worked at the Juneau Cold Storage before returning to Petersburg two years later. The couple raised six children; Amelia and Carol, a retired school teacher, were born after the war. Of their incarcerated children, their oldest son, Sam, Jr., became a leader in Alaska

Sam Kito, Jr., 2014.

Kito family: L. to R. Sam Kito, Jr., Amelia June, Saburo (father), Carol, Amelia (mother), Harry, Barbara & John, ca. 1954.

native and legislative affairs and served as president of the Alaska Federation of Natives. His sister Barbara resides in Petersburg, and his brother John is principal of Anchorage's Tyson Elementary School. Harry, born during incarceration at Camp Harmony, was killed while serving in Vietnam. A bridge in Petersburg now bears his name.

Mary Fukuyama had a long career with the Federal government in Washington, D.C., and then Seattle where she retired from the National Marine Fisheries Service in 1989. She died in 2014. Ethel Fukuyama returned to Seattle in 1956, married Toshio Terashita in 1958 and raised two children. She died in 2015. After graduating from high school in Washington, DC, Tom Fukuyama went on to receive an M.A. from the University of Washington, a Ph.D. in microbiology from the University of Pennsylvania and a Harvard fellowship. He became a professor at the University of Southern California, married Janet Tono in 1960 and raised three children. Tom died in 1993. Walter Fukuyama graduated from the University of Washington and Seattle University. He married Emiko Futori in 1947, and the couple raised two daughters. After retiring from the Boeing Company as a principle engineer in 1985, Walter studied at the Multnomah Bible College (now Multnomah University) in Portland, Oregon. Then he and Emiko spent four years as missionaries in Kobe, Japan. Walter's sister Ethel said her parents, deciding they were too old to restart their laundry in Juneau, re-settled in Seattle where they owned an apartment building and lived out their lives.

Walter Fukuyama, 2015.

When Bill Tanaka returned to Chicago, he married Toni Yamashiro and began work as an accountant by day while studying for his CPA degree by night. The couple raised two sons while Bill worked as a CPA and business manager for Chevron automobile dealerships in Los Angeles, Las Vegas and San Diego. He passed away in 2013. Alice Tanaka gradu-ated from San Jose State University

Bill Tanaka in his
City Café shirt, 1992.

Mary, Tom, and Walter Fukuyama, Ethel Fukuyama Terashita, 1985.

with a degree in occupational therapy. After her marriage to Katsumi "Kats" Hikido, the couple remained in San Jose and raised three sons. Mary Tanaka graduated from the University of Washington where she met her husband, Joe Abo. The couple settled in Bremerton,

Sisters Mary Tanaka Hikido and Alice Tanaka Abo and Jack Hermle visit Alice's grade school friend, Roberta Messerschmidt Spartz, 2013.

Washington, where Mary taught in the Bremerton School District and raised two children.

After his marriage to Jeanne Aoyama and receiving his medical degree as an anesthesiologist, John interned at Seattle's Virginia Mason Hospital. Positions at Seattle's Burien and Riverton hospitals followed. He then moved to Spokane and joined Anesthesia Associates PS. The couple raised five children, two of whom would also become doctors. In 1996, John was posthumously honored with the Distinguished Alumnus Award by the University Students Club at the University of Washington.

IN THEIR OWN WORDS

The first-person biographies, photographs, artifacts and artwork featured here figured prominently in a Juneau-Douglas City Museum exhibit which ran from June 2 through the end of October 2014 titled "The Forced Incarceration of Juneau's Japanese Community 1941-1951."

Kiichi (Henry) Akagi
by Randy Wanamaker and Connie Lundy

Kiichi Akagi, better known as "Henry," was born in Hiroshima, Japan, and came to Alaska at the turn of the century. He landed in Killisnoo near Angoon where he worked for the whaling station and herring saltery as a handy man and maintenance man. There were several Japanese there like the Samato Family. Some Japanese married Tlingits as did Henry who married Nellie Nelson and they had four children: William, Joseph, Connie and Frances. Nellie died soon after Frances was born around 1923, probably during the flu epidemic. Frances was adopted by a Tlingit family since Henry couldn't take care of her by himself. Later, Henry married Frannie Walters, but when she died, their child, Mary, was raised by her grandmother, Mary James. Connie died sometime in the 1930's.

The Akagi family lived in Killisnoo working in the salmon canneries around Hawk Inlet. Henry worked as an all-around handyman and maintenance man for the canneries. Although he never learned to speak Tlingit, he could understand it very well. He taught my father, Joseph, how to read and write Japanese when he was growing up.

When the evacuation order came in 1942, Henry and his son, William (26) were sent to different internment camps. Henry went to Santa Fe with other Alaskan men from Japan and William went to Minidoka with the mothers and American-born children. Henry's other son, Joseph, had already volunteered for the army in 1937 when he was 19 and was serving under General Patton in North Africa. In 1943, security officers from the War Department came to Joseph and told him to sign the Loyalty Oath. He questioned why he had to because he

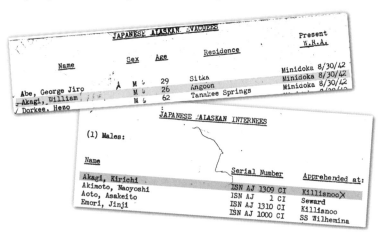

William Akagi (top) is listed on the Non-Alien Japanese Alaskan Evacuees List, and Kiichi Akagi (bottom) is listed as "Kirichi" on the Alien Japanese Alaskan Internees List in documents issued by the Western Defense Command.

The Akagi Family in Nobu Tanaka's Garden, 1957. Left to right: Sam, Henry, Nobu, Eunice, Pamela, and Joseph. Image provided by the Akagi family.

told them he was raised a Tlingit. His commanding officer stood up for him, so Joseph didn't have to sign anything. When officers came later to send Joseph to the 442nd all Japanese-American Regiment, he declined staying he wanted to stay with his 7th Infantry Regiment, 3rd Infantry Division. His commanding officer spoke up for him again, so he was allowed to serve with his unit until he was discharged in 1946.

After the war, Joseph married my mother, Eunice Wanamaker, so then Joseph became my stepfather and Henry, my step grandfather. My father went to diesel school under the GI Bill. After he finished his training, our family traveled with him all over Alaska, United States and Canada where he worked for fish canneries as a diesel mechanic and port engineer. We spent many summers in the Killisnoo area. When our family lived in Seattle, I remember we visited Uncle William in the hospital when he was sick with cancer. He was always happy to see us children. He passed away around 1952. When my grandfather had a few strokes, he came to live with us in Seattle and Juneau, but he always went back to his own home in Killisnoo where he eventually died.

Although I knew my grandfather had a family in Hiroshima he used to write to, he never heard from them again after the war started. I remember he had many Japanese books and magazines and calendars with pictures of mountains, probably Fujiyama, and pagodas in his house. He kept a large garden and put up his own food to live on during the winter. When he saw me running around the town, he'd ask me where I was going and gave me quarters to go to the movies and buy candy and pop to share with the other kids. He liked to talk to the Japanese fish buyers who came to the canneries for salmon eggs. They got a kick out of hearing my grandfather call his dog, "Koo-kuh-ten," a Tlingit name, because they thought it sounded Japanese. That dog went everywhere my grandfather went and was his faithful companion.

My grandfather was a modest man, never overly flattering, and polite. He liked to dress properly when he went to town or received visitors by wearing a business suit, tie and hat. He also wore a mustache as long as I can remember. I don't remember him or William ever talking about the internment camps. I don't even remember my father talking much about being in the Army either. I learned about some of his experiences from listening to him talk to men who served with him.

Hikohachi Fukuyama

by Nancy (Fukuyama) Albright

My grandfather, Walter Hikohachi Fukuyama, came from Hiratsuka, Kanagawa Prefecture, Japan to Canada and then to Juneau in 1903. He worked at the Treadwell Mine and then in Judge Gunnison's house as a house-boy where he practiced his English and learned to cook American food. Eventually, he joined three other Japanese men who ran a laundry. In 1920, he wed Mume Iida from Chigasaki, Kanagawa Prefecture in an arranged marriage. Around 1929, with help from the First National Bank, my grandfather became the sole owner of the Juneau Laundry and built one of Juneau's first cement structures that still exists on Franklin Street.

My grandparents had four children: Mary (1921), Ethel (1922), my father, Walter (1924) and Thomas (1927). The Fukuyama kids said they had an idyllic upbringing in Juneau. Their parents might have told another story with early mornings and late nights tending to family and laundry business. My father and Uncle Tom skied, hunted, fished, and played along Gold Creek and in the mountains. My Aunt Mary and Ethel were busy with school clubs and activities, fishing and picking blueberries. My aunts graduated from Juneau High School, and my father played and lettered in basketball there. Aunt Mary, the eldest, was sent to Japan to learn about the culture as was the custom for some Japanese families. She also attended Waseda University and lived with family in Hiratsuka. She had a hard time there as she was not used to the strict Japanese behavior that the family expected of her.

Mary Fukuyama wearing a kimono in Japan, 1939.

On December 7, 1941, the Fukuyama world turned upside down when the Japanese bombed Pearl Harbor. Aunt Mary was "trapped" in Japan, not being able to return home. My grandfather was taken under guard to jail where he was interrogated and then shipped away with other Japanese men in Juneau to Seattle. From there he was sent by train to a Department of Justice camp in Lordsburg and then Santa Fe, New Mexico. My grandmother and her children were sent to Minidoka Internment Camp in Hunt, Idaho, where the land and climate was very different from Juneau.

My grandfather was not able to join his family for two years. The family had no privacy, as they lived with other families in tarpaper barracks with only thin plywood walls separating the one-room living quarters. Barbed wire fences surrounded the grounds with soldiers guarding from watch towers. My father said he had never seen so many Japanese people in one place. While in camp, my grandmother attended Christian services and was given a Bible written in Japanese. She gave her life to Jesus in Minidoka. That was very significant, as both our grandparents' families were Buddhist. Although, it was a gradual process, all of their children have since become Christians as well as our own.

After the family was released from camp, they scattered to various locations. Aunt Mary was able to return to the states. She and Aunt Ethel and Uncle Tom moved to Washington, D.C. where they found work with the U.S. Government and Tom finished high school. My father, who graduated from high school in Minidoka, was drafted and assigned to the Military Intelligence Service (MIS). He was stationed in Tokyo during the occupation of Japan. He met and married my mother, Emiko, while stationed there.

Torao and Tooru Kanazawa

by Mark Kanazawa
with background information from
Sushi and Sourdough and *Pacific Citizen*

When Tooru Kanazawa wrote his autobiographic novel, *Sushi and Sourdough*, about growing up in Douglas and Juneau, Alaska, in the mid 1900's, he created hardy characters of Torao, his brother ("Ken"), as well as himself ("Fuse").

Their father, Matajiro Kanazawa, left Japan as a young man in the late 1880's to seek his fortune in the Klondike where he earned enough to return to his village in Yonezawa and bring his wife, Yaso, and two sons, Torao (16) and Miyoshi (14), to America. He brought his young family to Spokane, Washington, where Tooru was born in 1906.

After listening to his father tell of his adventures in Alaska, Torao made his way to Alaska, first to Cordova and then to Douglas, where he worked at the Treadwell Mine. Since the mine was doing so well with over 2000 workers, Torao persuaded his parents to come north in 1912 to open a bath house and

Tooru and Masaka Kanazawa wedding portrait, 1948.

barbershop for the miners in Douglas. Torao helped his father support their family, which had now grown to six children with the addition of brother Tetsuo in 1908 and younger sisters Misao and Kiyoko, born in 1910 and 1912.

When the Treadmill Mine collapsed in 1917, Torao lost his job along with most of the miners, but he found another as a waiter at the City Cafe owned by Shonosuke Tanaka in Juneau. Everyone in town knew Torao as "Bobby." When their parents returned to Japan because of their father's ill health, Torao took on the responsibility of making sure Tooru got a good education.

In 1922, Torao stayed behind when Tooru moved to Seattle to attend Franklin High School and then the University of Washington where he received a B.A. in journalism. After graduating, Tooru moved to Los Angeles to work for the Japanese-American newspaper *Rafu Shimpo*, putting his journalism degree to good use. While there, he covered the 1932 Summer Olympic Games for the newspaper. However, that job didn't last because of the Depression.

Tooru then moved back to Juneau to rejoin Torao and drove a delivery truck for Fukuyama's Juneau Laundry while still continuing to pursue his dreams by writing and selling stories to such outlets as the *Christian Science Monitor* and *Thrilling Sports*. By 1939, he was able to move to New York doing freelance writing before taking a job with Mike Masaoka at the office of the Japanese American Citizens League.

After Japan bombed Pearl Harbor in 1941, the Japanese in Juneau were given orders to be shipped out to internment camps. By this time, Torao, in his 50's, was the only one of his family left in Alaska and in ill health. On the Army's list of "internees," he's noted with both his Japanese and American names, "Torao Bob Kanazawa." He was sent to Lordsburg, New Mexico, as were most Isseis (first generation Japanese) who were then later transferred to Santa Fe. While in Lordsburg, Torao died. Tooru later told his family that his brother's spirit was crushed in camp.

In 1943, Tooru volunteered to serve with the newly formed 442nd Regimental Combat Team. At thirty-six years of age, he was one of the oldest enlisted soldiers in the unit. He served with distinction in Italy and France, earning a Bronze Star for meritorious service as a radioman.

After the war, Tooru returned to New York, where he married Masako Fuji in 1948. Their daughter, Teru, was born in 1950, and then son, Mark, and another daughter, Joy, were born in 1955 and 1958. During the early years of their marriage, Tooru served as the English language editor for the *Hokubei Shimpo*, later the *Nichibei*. To support his growing family, he worked as a travel agent for the New York Travel Service where he became vice president and retired in 1987 at the ripe old age of 80.

Tooru never gave up on his dreams of being a published author and around 1970, he began to write again. His family recalled him rising at 5:30 and writing for two hours before going off to work in the morning, day after day, week after week. The result was *Sushi and Sourdough*, published in 1989. He continued to write until the very end of his life.

Saburo (Sam, Sr.) Kito
by Sam Kito, Jr.

My father, Saburo Kito, (Sam, Sr.) came from Osaka in the early 1900's to Petersburg. There he met my mother, Amelia (Okegawa), whose mother was Tlingit and father was Japanese. Both my mother and father worked for Kaylor Dahl and the Knute Thompson canneries. There was a large community of Japanese families besides ours in Petersburg: Kawashima, Ozawa, Kaino, Komatsubara, Ohashi and Oyama.

On my father's side, there was our family and his brother, Tom Kito, and his wife, Lucy, and their children. On my mother's side, there was her father, Harry Okegawa, and her brother George, and his wife, Irene, and their children.

After Pearl Harbor, I was only five years old when my whole family was evacuated from Petersburg, and that included Barbara ((3) and John (1) and my Uncle Tom. Also evacuated were my mother's father and brother. Uncle Tom's wife, Lucy, had the option of staying with their children because she was Tlingit. Although my mother also had the option of staying, he decided to go thinking my father would be with us. She was pregnant at the time. I can barely remember going away on a ship to Seattle. After we got to Camp Harmony at the Puyallup Fairgrounds in Seattle my brother Harry was born.

All the men in my family were separated from us and sent to camp in Santa Fe along with the other Alaskan men who came from Japan. The families were all sent to Minidoka. We didn't see our father for about three years. I can't remember too much about camp, but I do remember I had a friend, Kenny Arai, who died there of a brain tumor. I learned from reading the, *Minidoka Interlude*, that our family lived in barrack #3 of twelve barracks in Block 24. There were six rooms in each barrack for six families with only cots and a pot belly stove. My mother, myself, Barbara, John and Harry are in a group picture showing everyone living in our block.

Kito extended family in Juneau after returning from Minidoka, 1946. From left to right, 2nd row: John Kito, Barbara Kito. Harry Kito sitting on far right of front row.

After the war, my father worked at Anderson Dam near Jerome, Idaho. From there, my family moved to Juneau around 1946 for about two years. I went to the public schools, but was able to play with the St. Anne Cardinals basketball team even though we weren't Catholics. Some of my classmates were Don Abel, Johnny Ebona, and David Hollingsworth. My mother worked at the City Cafe and my father worked at the Juneau Cold Storage for Elton Engstrom.

When we moved back to Petersburg, we were met by our good friends John and Ann Kolstrand, who had taken care of our property for us. Our family grew with the addition of Carol and Amelia Jane. I stayed in Petersburg until I graduated from high school. I joined the marines and afterwards went to school to become a communications specialist. I ended up working at the NASA satellite tracking station in Fairbanks and I became active in the Fairbanks Native Association and the Alaska Native Claims Settlement Act (ANCSA).

Sam Kito standing next to pot belly stove on a Minidoka Pilgrimage, 2003.

I don't remember my parents talking about Minidoka except to say, "It was a tough time." My youngest daughter, Hope, read about the Minidoka Pilgrimages and said she wanted to go, so we went in 2003. It was very hot there. We saw the barracks, the few standing landmarks and the barren land which is now a National Historic Monument. She's glad we went there together and now we both know what it was like.

Haruo Kumasaka
by Haruo Kumasaka

I came to Juneau when I was 22 years old. In 1939, Tooru Kanazawa wanted to leave his job at the Juneau Laundry so he wrote to me in Seattle and asked if I would like to take his place. Mr. Fukuyama needed more workers so I wrote to Sam Taguchi to come up and we shared a room above the Juneau Laundry. I knew Sam because we played baseball together in Seattle. I drove the laundry's brand new delivery wagon to pick up and deliver laundry and Sam operated the washing machines. Sam always sent half of his paycheck to his mother who was a widow raising her five children alone.

Most of the Japanese laundry workers ran a $1 tab for all three meals at the City Cafe. You could order anything off the menu like boiled salmon belly with drawn butter, and you could ask for rice. Lunchtime was pretty busy, and Tanaka never wrote down the orders that Kono, the waiter, would call out like, "Beef stew pair, roast pork same time." He didn't like to talk, but this laundry worker wanted to talk to him about something, maybe complain about the food. Tanaka told him, "Don't talk!" After that, the worker got mad and never came back.

Sam and I played baseball for the Elks Team, but we couldn't go inside the Elks Lodge because of the color code at the time. Other teammates were Max Lewis and Molly McSpadden. Sam, Max, Ross Vories, the Nielsens (Emma, Louise, Jim and Ed) and I liked going to the Resurrection Lutheran Church. We joined the young people's group and went fishing and ice skating and had a good time.

I joined the National Guard in 1940 with Max and we reported once a week to do drills. We became good friends because we both liked to ski. Max had come to Juneau when his sister married into the Gross family who owned the Capital Theater. On a furlough in 1941, Max and I went to Olympia to visit his father who was sculptor

114

laureate for the state of Washington. He showed us his "Winged Victory" monument there on the capitol grounds.

On December 7, 1941, I took Tom Fukuyama to the Douglas ski trail. As we were walking across the Douglas Bridge back to Juneau, all hell broke out in town because we heard Japan bombed Pearl Harbor. Since there was no air service, people started sending boats of women and children to the states while the fathers stayed in Juneau. The Civil Defense enforced blackout at night. Soldiers were sent to Juneau to build an air strip. So many soldiers came, the laundries became very busy washing their clothes.

Ham Kumasaka in Juneau, 1939.

Since Mr. Fukuyama was jailed along with the other Japanese Isseis (Japanese born), he put Sam and me in charge of shutting down the laundry. We knew we were going

Ham and Minnie Kumasaka, 1990.

to be evacuated, too, because of President Roosevelt's Executive Order. In April 1942, Sam and I went to the special graduation assembly at the high school for John Tanaka. I couldn't hold back my tears. I knew how John and his friend, Skip McKinnon, got their fathers to chip in some money to help put out the 1942 school annual because there was no money otherwise.

Just before we shipped out, Reverend Hillerman taught catechism to Sam and me. On Good Friday 1942, Sam and I were baptized. The whole congregation came up to us afterwards to congratulate us. After we arrived in Minidoka, I was able to join my family.

Sometime in 1944, I was allowed to leave Minidoka for Chicago with others to study or work. Before going there, I took a bus to visit my father in Lordsburg, New Mexico. When I got there, I was told by the guards that I could only visit for two hours, once in the morning and once in the afternoon and I had to speak English. I was sent to the post office to wait there for my father. My father was called out to go to the post office because he thought he had some mail. When he saw me, he couldn't believe his eyes. I had to say, "Haruo desu" (I'm Haruo). The guard told him, "You're supposed to speak English!" The next day, I asked to see Tanaka and Fukuyama and my father, too. But since I could only talk to two people at a time, Tanaka stood apart but kept edging closer and closer. Pretty soon, the guard let all three of us visit.

I stayed in Chicago and got married to Minnie Ota. I worked for Noma, a Christmas tree light company, all my life and eventually became vice president. We moved back to Seattle around 2000 to be with family. Even though I'm now 94 years old, I still remember Juneau as a real adventure for me. Ed. Note: Haruo "Ham" Kumasaka passed away on February 21, 2014 at age 95.

Sam and Gim Taguchi

Compiled from Reiko (Taguchi) Sumada, the *Juneau Empire* and a 1990 interview by Ron Inouye, *Alaska's Japanese Research Project.*

After her husband, Seike, died, Matsuye Taguchi was left at age forty to support her family of five (Kimi, Sam, Susumu, Gim and Reiko) by selling vegetables at Pike Place Public Market. All the children pitched in and learned the meaning of hard work from her. Yet, Sumada said her mother was a "huge baseball fan and never missed her boys' games." When Sam was in his twenties, he came to Juneau to work at the Juneau Laundry with his friend, Ham Kumasaka, and sent part of his earnings to his mother.

Sam said he first heard the news about Japan's bombing Pearl Harbor in a movie theater. "When I heard about it, I said, 'I don't believe any of those things.'" When the town learned that all the Japanese in Juneau would be evacuated in April, the high school arranged a special commencement service for John Tanaka. "Everybody was happy to see that," Sam said. The night before evacuation, he and Ham visited friends who were sorry to see them go. "They were just about as much put out as we were." They were shipped out at 10:00 at night, stopping at Petersburg, Wrangell and Ketchikan to pick up other Japanese on the way to Seattle.

After landing in Seattle, they were taken to Puyallup Fairgrounds barracks where Sam said he saw grass growing through the floor. Since he didn't like the Vienna sausages they served in the mess hall, he ate so much bread that his friends started calling him "Bread." A few months later they were taken to Minidoka, a place Sam described as "a lot of sagebrush, flat and hot and pretty miserable." There he was able to join the rest of his family from Seattle, except for his sister, Kimi, a nurse working

Taguchi family portrait, 1928. Left to right, 3rd row: Kimi, Seike; 2nd row: Sam, Susumu; 1st row: Matsuye, Reiko, Gim.

at a Catholic Hospital in Rochester, Minnesota. Sumada said their family of five "shared one room with a pot-bellied stove, five cots and nothing else but soon made comfortable with her mother's sewing skills." At first, Sam worked in the camp laundry; then with his brothers, Susumu and Gim, picked potatoes or topped sugar beets for farmers nearby.

When some internees were allowed to leave the camps, Sam joined his sister, Kimi, in Rochester. Later he moved to Chicago and worked at a pinball factory. Although his brother Susumu and Gim were drafted in 1944, Sam was not called up. Gim joined the Military Intelligence Service and served in post-war Japan as an interpreter. After V-J (Victory over Japan) Day, Gim toured Japan on a goodwill baseball team that included some New York Yankees. Gim then moved to Chicago to stay with Sam.

Sam came back to Juneau in 1949 when John Tanaka asked if he would join Katsutaro Komatsubara in partnership with his father, Shonosuke Tanaka, to run the City Cafe before he left for college. Sam took care of the books and worked as the day waiter. In 1951, he called Gim from Chicago to work as a night cook and waiter. Gim fit right in with the sports crowd by playing for the Juneau Imperials and the City Cafe teams and was inducted into the 1955 Gold Medal Basketball Hall of Fame.

The brothers combined their interest in sports and politics with work. They ran the City Cafe like a 24-hour talk show where games and politics were analyzed and argued over cups of coffee. Sam sometimes purposely overfilled cups as his test to see if people could take a joke. Rudy Ripley wrote, "Some customers actually felt slighted if they didn't receive an insult during their visit. It had become a badge of acceptance." After the City Cafe closed in the 1970's, customers convinced Sam and Gim to come out of retirement to open Taguchi's Fine Chow.

Sam was appointed Grand Marshal for the 1989 Fourth of July Parade and as honorary Commissioner of Athletics for the State of Alaska by Governor Bill Egan. In the interview with Inouye, Sam said that when he came back to Juneau in 1949, "I thought I'd just stay a couple

Sam at the (new) City Cafe, 1960. (Photo by Mark Kelly, *Juneau Empire*, March 9, 2005.)

years, but I'm still here." In 1992 when Sam was undergoing cancer treatments, he wrote an open letter of appreciation to all who had written cards and letters to him. He wrote, "They must be the nicest people in the world and I love them all."

Shonosuke Tanaka
by Alice (Tanaka) Hikido

My father, Shonosuke Tanaka, immigrated to the U.S. from Japan in 1900. Around 1912 he settled in Juneau and opened the City Café on South Franklin. He returned to Japan in 1922 and married my mother, Nobu Fujita, in a marriage arranged by their families. They had five children, John, William, Teddy, Alice and Mary. We were all born in Juneau. Teddy passed away in 1939.

I was in the fourth grade when World War II started on Sunday, Dec. 7, 1941. The next day I reluctantly went to school, apprehensive of the reaction of my classmates. I returned home to find FBI agents searching our home. When they were finished, they took my father with them. We learned that he was put in jail with other men who were born in Japan. Later they were then sent to a camp in New Mexico. This was a fearful time for us, especially for my mother who had always depended upon my father and couldn't understand English very well.

The rest of our family soon learned that we would share a similar fate. Bill and John, still in high school, closed the family restaurant and prepared for our departure. The school presented John's diploma to him in a special assembly. In April, we were given less than 24 hours to board a military transport ship. Our destination was the Puyallup Fairgrounds near Seattle, Washington, which had been transformed into a temporary assembly camp. Bill's good friend, Tony Del Santo, who had just moved from Juneau to Seattle, wrote and said that he and his mother would visit him on a certain day. We eagerly went to the main gate to see them. They had to remain on the other side of the gate, but Tony's mother somehow passed over this wonderful homemade chocolate cake. While we were at Puyallup, we learned that John's senior class honored him at their graduation ceremony by leaving an empty

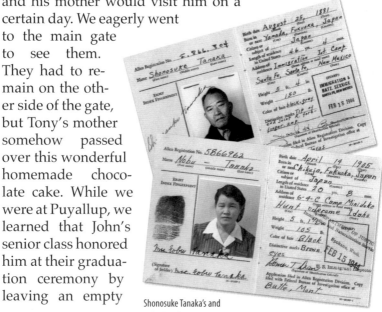

Shonosuke Tanaka's and Nobu Tanaka's Alien Registration Cards for Evacuation, 1942.

chair for him, their class valedictorian. Both of these acts of support boosted our spirits.

In the summer, we were sent to the Minidoka Camp in Idaho, our final destination. The camp was surrounded by a barbwire fence with guard towers, a stark reminder that we were prisoners. Finally in 1944, our father was transferred to Minidoka and reunited with us. When the war ended in 1945, John was serving in the Army, and Bill had taken advantage of the loosening restrictions and had gone to work in Chicago.

My father and mother decided to return to Juneau. I was now twelve and eager to go home again, but Mary at five had no memory of Juneau. The Tanner family, our friends for many years, met our ship as we docked and invited us to stay at their Scandinavian Rooms across from the City Cafe until we could move back into our home. My father took out a loan from the B.M. Behrends Bank and made preparation to restart the City Café. Bill returned from Chicago

Bill and Mary Tanaka in front of City Cafe, 1946.

to help my father and together they opened the cafe for business in 1946. Later that year, John was discharged from the army and added his effort. Other friends, John Hermle of the Home Grocery and George Messerschmidt of the San Francisco Bakery, extended credit until the City Café was able to pay their bills again. Very importantly, old faithful customers returned. This was a testimony of the supportive community of Juneau.

The interior of the second City Cafe when it relocated across the street from the original site, 1960.

It was good to have the war years behind us. By 1950, my father had paid off the loan and entered into partnership with Katsutaro Komatsubara and Sam Taguchi. The three of them operated the City Café together until my father passed away in 1957.

Why do we tell our stories?

"We usually tell them because we want to be remembered long after we are gone. I often think about a Buddhist priest who asked my family at a memorial service, "Do you remember walking up the steps to the temple? If you remember, the steps exist. If you don't remember, they don't." He said taking the time to remember was the purpose of the memorial service. If we don't remember our incarceration, it is like it never happened. Research shows that the more our children know and remember about their family, the more tools they have to face life. It is important to know the many ups and downs family members have faced (because) shared stories mean shared lives."

– Mary Abo speaking at the Minidoka Pilgrimage, 2015.

Art and Artifacts

Fumi Matsumoto

Fumi Matsumoto has lived and taught art in Fairbanks and Juneau for the past 33 years. Born in Japan, Fumi's family came to the United States in 1952 when she was four years old, and she grew up in Berkeley, California. Always influenced by Japanese culture and history, much of her art reflects the Japanese aesthetic and often the Japanese American experience.

Fumi has strong emotional ties to the work she submitted for the exhibit. Much of it incorporates images of her family members and her personal history. Her father was incarcerated in the Jerome Relocation Center in Arkansas, then volunteered for the Army where he served in Burma with Merrill's Marauders. He received the Congressional Medal of Honor in 2011 for saving the lives of fellow marauders.

Fumi uses recycled and found objects in her mixed media pieces and often uses Japanese techniques such as raku ceramics, sumi ink painting, origami (paper folding), kirigami (paper cutting), handmade paper and block printing. She said, "I continue to be inspired by the struggles of past generations of Japanese Americans and their ability to endure hardships as well as appreciate their successes." Here Fumi describes two pieces used in the exhibit. They are followed by some of the exhibit's artifacts. (Photos on pages 124 & 125 courtesy of Fumi).

I made "Ibara no Michi" while I was on San Juan Island off the coast of Washington when I had no studio or equipment. Because commercial art supplies were difficult to obtain, many internees made beautiful works of art in the camps using only the limited materials they could find in their environment. I came across a patch of Nootka Rose growing along the cliffs overlooking the sea and was struck by the dark red branches covered with thorns. I took some and crafted a lattice by weaving the prickly branches with my bare hands and tied off the ends with some dried blades of grass. It was impossible to avoid the thorns and my fingertips bled from the punctures. I also folded ten origami cranes with used teabags and placed them on the thorny branches. The name of an internment camp is written in Japanese on the back of each crane. My mother suggested the title, which translates to "Pathway of Thorns." The sculpture reflects the life of hardship in the harsh, isolated desert environments where the Japanese were forced to live.

"Minidoka Interlude" shows a photo of a young Japanese woman, my mother, in a kimono behind a wooden window frame. Artifacts encased in a wire cage represent life in camp. They include a photo of a Nisei soldier, my father, who like many young men, left family and friends behind in camp when they enlisted in the United States Army to fight and defend their country. Shells, bones and barbed wire are scattered on the floor of the wire cage along with a map of the Minidoka barracks and a scroll containing the names of the many individuals living there. I wanted to convey a sense of desolation in a remote desert location, but also the "gaman" spirit of endurance that the Japanese Americans possessed.

1942 Juneau High School *Totem* cover copied from a Tlingit blanket design. John Tanaka worked on it as co-editor of the yearbook.

Greasewood vase made during incarceration by Shonosuke Tanaka.

Greasewood bridge made during incarceration by Shonosuke Tanaka.

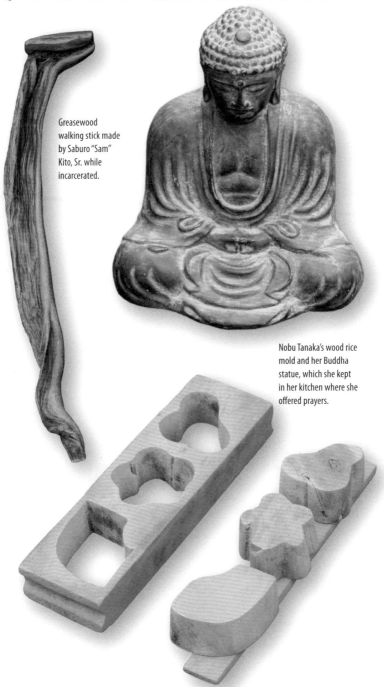

Greasewood walking stick made by Saburo "Sam" Kito, Sr. while incarcerated.

Nobu Tanaka's wood rice mold and her Buddha statue, which she kept in her kitchen where she offered prayers.

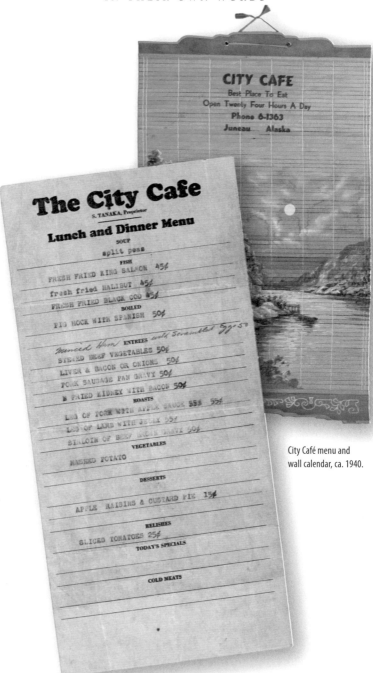

CITY CAFE
Best Place To Eat
Open Twenty Four Hours A Day
Phone 6-1363
Juneau   Alaska

The City Cafe
S. TANAKA, Proprietor

Lunch and Dinner Menu

SOUP
split peas

FISH
FRESH FRIED KING SALMON 45¢

fresh fried HALIBUT 45¢

FRESH FRIED BLACK COD 45¢

BOILED
PIG HOCK WITH SPANISH 50¢

Minced Ham ### ENTREES with Scrambled Eggs 50
STEWED BEEF VEGETABLES 50¢

LIVER & BACON OR ONIONS 50¢

PORK SAUSAGE PAN GRAVY 50¢

B FRIED KIDNEY WITH BACON 50¢

ROASTS
LEG OF PORK WITH APPLE SAUCE 55¢ 55¢

LEG OF LAMB WITH JELLY 55¢

SIRLOIN OF BEEF BROWN GRAVY 50¢

VEGETABLES
MASHED POTATO

DESSERTS

APPLE RAISINS & CUSTARD PIE 15¢

RELISHES
SLICED TOMATOES 25¢

TODAY'S SPECIALS

COLD MEATS

City Café menu and
wall calendar, ca. 1940.

Laundry bag and towel used at
the Juneau Laundry, ca. 1940

Mume Fukuyama's Bible. Mume converted to Christianity while she was incarcerated.

Vintage suitcase, ca. 1940, filled with folded origami cranes. Suitcase provided by Marjorie Shackelford.

SEEKING JUSTICE:
THE EMPTY CHAIR MEMORIAL

Despite a national pardon and reparations, the story of Japanese American incarceration during World War II remained large-ly an unknown event to the general public. When the Tanakas returned to Juneau after the war and reopened the City Café, which became a thriving eatery well known and frequented by the local populace, it came something of a shock for following generations to gradually realize that the Tanakas, Taguchis, Fukuyamas and Komatsubaras had been imprisoned during the war. As that knowledge grew, a small group of locals decided to acknowledge what had happened in the way of a memorial to honor those who had been taken. What follows is the story, by the author, of how the Empty Chair Memorial was created. It is testimony to how a community, once its citizens knew the injustice of a grievous wrong, decided to do something about it, even if the event happened many years ago, even if the attempt was small in comparison to the gravity of the incarceration.

The idea for a memorial to recognize the Japanese Americans who were taken from Juneau during World War II crystalized with a familiar name discovered in a book during the summer of 2010. My sister Margie, visiting Juneau from her home in Fresno, California, was with me at Betty Marriott's home listening to a P.E.O. sponsored presentation about her family's incarceration at Minidoka Relocation Center. Margie was quietly leafing through a book published by Minidoka incarcerees, *Minidoka Interlude*, when she discovered some familiar Juneau names among a list of more than 9,000 people. One of them belonged to her childhood friend Mary Tanaka Abo. She slipped the book onto my lap, her index finger pointing to Mary's name. It was a galvanizing moment for us.

We knew a little bit about that unfortunate period in United States history. Margie had told me that after decades of silence, Mary had begun talking about her family's incarceration. Meanwhile, I had read *Nisei: The Quiet Americans* by Bill Hosokawa about the government's unconstitutional treatment of Japanese citizens during World War II. Learning what Mary and her family had suffered so long ago was shocking to Margie and reprehensible to both of us. But seeing the printed names was a defining moment that began a four-year quest for some kind of justice.

Following Betty's presentation, we began talking in earnest. I knew plaques were placed on Japanese American homes in Hood River, Oregon, to commemorate their incarceration, but as far as I knew, nothing had been done to honor those taken from Juneau. I thought there should at least be a plaque to honor them, too. We agreed; yes, something should be done. On her way back to Fresno, Margie stopped in Washington to visit Mary, and together they visited the Bainbridge Island Japanese American Exclusion Memorial where they viewed the inspirational result of that community's efforts to recognize the incarceration of their Japanese Americans.

Meanwhile, I pursued local knowledge about the event. After checking with Juneau-Douglas City Museum Director Jane Lindsey and Juneau historian Marie Darlin, I learned there had never been local recognition regarding the forced removal of Juneau Japanese Americans. Coincidentally, Marie told me she had accumulated a file of information about the local event that she wanted to share. When Margie visited the following August 2011, we discovered that Marie, from the Juneau High School class of 1943, knew Mary's brother John Tanaka. She said he had been valedictorian for his class of 1942. However, she said John had been forcibly removed from Juneau, along with all Japanese Americans in town, before the actual graduation occurred. She said John's class had left an empty chair to honor him and, by extension, all those taken. "I've been saving this file because I've always felt something should be done about that event," she said.

Marie then directed us to the Alaska State Historical Museum, which she said housed the original typed transcripts from oral interviews of incarcerees profiled in the book *Alaska's Japanese Pioneers--Faces, Voices, Stories: A Synopsis of Oral History Transcripts* by Ron Inouye, Carol Hoshiko and Kazumi Heshiki. The book, part of Alaska's Japanese Pioneer Project, included interviews with former Juneau residents Sam Taguchi and Walter Fukuyama. Marie loaned us her copy of the book and also steered us to the Juneau Historical Resource Committee, of which she was a member, about the idea of creating a memorial.

After reviewing the transcripts, Margie and I walked the docks near where the Tanaka family's City Café was once located and discussed placing a memorial plaque in that area. Margie visited the Alaska State Library to search World War II era newspaper files and began compiling her own file. She told me, "It was the visit to Marie's that inspired the empty chair. I remember you writing those words in red letters on the file folder you gave me and asking, 'Is this what you want to call it?' and my saying, 'Yes, this is a wonderful metaphor for what we'd like to do.'" Thus, the idea for an empty chair project was born.

The Empty Chair Committee

For the next step, Margie gathered former Juneau High School classmates David Gray, Janie Homan and Dixie Belcher to share her information and to ask if their class of 1958 could sponsor the memorial. She discovered she was not alone in her point of view and began forming a committee. When Margie approached Mary with the plan, she found her surprised and pleased that her classmates and friends wanted to honor the empty chair event. We were pleased, too, because the quest to uncover this part of Juneau's history would first center on the City Cafe and the Tanaka family, who would then lead us to information about other Japanese American families. We were fortunate to have such primary sources as Mary, and her sister, Alice Hikido, who could remember the Japanese Americans mentioned in this book. It became my goal to fit all the pieces together.

At the next gathering, Margie's classmates Jan and Andy Pekovich and my husband, Roger, and I (class of 1960) joined the group. The new committee, with Margie as chair, quickly expanded with Alice (class of 1950), Marie Darlin (class of 1943), Jackie Triplette (class of 1961), Marsha Bennett (class of 1958) and Betty Marriott. By default, the Grummett home became the coordinating headquarters between Margie in California, Mary in Washington, Alice in California and the committee in Juneau. The project would require several trips to Juneau by Margie and Mary during the next three years, with business conducted and developed primarily through email correspondence.

By fall, Mary and Margie began conceiving the idea of something more substantial than a plaque for the memorial. Margie said, "I felt the image of a chair, like the empty chair used at the actual graduation, seemed more powerful than a plaque." That thought eventually morphed into a solitary, wood-slatted, folding chair indicative of the event's era. The friends envisioned incarceree names and a narrative about the event placed somewhere on the memorial. Alice compiled a list of Juneau incarcerees from the National Archives, and the committee began looking for grant and public art sources to fund the project. In November, Alice shared a video from an oral history project created by the San Leandro Library in California titled *In the Same Boat*. It is an eloquent seven-minute narration by Alice about the experience of being taken via an Army transport, along with Japanese Americans from other Southeast Alaska towns, to a temporary detention center in Puyallup, Washington, and from there to the Minidoka incarceration site in Idaho. The video would be the touchstone of future presentations to local organizations. Wherever it was shown, the room stilled.

The next step was to select a memorial artist, who could also provide a visual concept of the chair for public presentations. Mary asked her college friend and artist Patti Warashina for a reference, preferably someone familiar with public art who could replicate a chair for the project. Patti suggested Seattle artist Peter Reiquam. At their initial meeting in Peter's studio, Mary said, "I brought the photo of a wooden folding chair. He thought the chair was a great idea, but he suggested that the chair be oversized to make a more powerful statement." With Peter's enthusiasm and agreement to create the memorial, the project moved forward in earnest.

The following May 2012, Margie, with Mary and other members of the committee attending, presented a proposal to the Juneau Historical Resource Committee in Juneau's City Hall for creating the Empty Chair Memorial. Following the presentation, the historical committee endorsed the project. Soon publicity about the memorial arrived on the pages of the *Juneau Empire* in one of several articles to be written by Melissa Griffiths, which generated local interest. Dennis Harris, whose parents had been friends with John Tanaka wrote to Margie saying, "I think that an empty chair would be a fitting memorial, and I think that a fitting site would be Capital School Park, which is next to the building that was the high school that John attended." Serving then as City and Borough of Juneau Planning Manager, Greg Chaney also suggested the park as an alternative memorial location, since the dock area had become more commercialized and, he felt, less local. As an independent filmmaker, Greg was very interested in the project and agreed to become an advisory member of the committee. He would subsequently create a documentary called *The Empty Chair*, which was based on videotaped interviews of surviving incarcerees and others familiar with the event.

Upon surveying the park, the former site of their grade school, with its twin, the former Juneau High School building still standing in the lot next to it, members of the Empty Chair Committee agreed that the park should be the memorial's home if approved by the city. The chosen

Artist Peter Reiquam's rendering of the Empty Chair Memorial.

site sat atop a small rise in a corner of the park's greenbelt. Though we couldn't articulate it at the time, Margie did so later at the dedication when she spoke about the "sheltering backdrop of Mt. Juneau." She said, "Though the city of Juneau itself may have changed in many aspects since 1942, Mt. Juneau has not. To me this mountain is a steadfast companion in a shared past whose memories still echo down through 72 years of Juneau history and reverberate into the present." She spoke to other feelings we experienced at the site, about how the memorial would face Gastineau Channel and "the ever-changing vista of Juneau. It has the potential to educate and influence the future. For although we wish to honor the past, it's the future of our children and grand-children we also want to affect."

The summer brought numerous developments. Roger, Marie, Betty Marriott and I attended the City of Juneau's second Capital Park Master Plan Design meeting where we received enthusiastic encouragement from the city ar-chitect, park superintendent and the Parks and Recreation Advisory Committee (PRAC) chairman. We were told that our preferred memorial site was least likely to be changed over time. The project also subsequently received en-dorsements from the Juneau-Douglas School District and the Juneau-Douglas City Museum.

In July, Peter sent his preliminary memorial proposal, which included a sketched design of a bronze chair that he felt would invite interaction from visitors to the park. It sat on a base reminiscent of a gym floor. He wrote, "The floorboards appear to have been ripped directly from the floor of the building – a metaphor for the innocent people who were ripped from the security and comfort of their community." The narrative of the empty chair event, the names of those incarcerated and the Japanese symbol for peace, Heiwa, to honor the language of the Issei, were shown etched into the chair's base.

Other developments picked up speed. I presented in-formation about the memorial at the July PRAC meeting, and another procedural step was achieved. The Empty Chair Project's finance committee also strategized, and Roger reported that the Juneau Community Foundation had accepted the Empty Chair Project under its auspices, relieving the committee of the arduous process of creat-ing a nonprofit status. Nancy DeCherney at the Juneau Arts and Humanities Council agreed to help facilitate those funds. Also that July, Margie launched the Empty Chair's website www.emptychairproject.wordpress.com with the guidance of Andy Abo, Mary Abo's son. Then, with the help of her nine-year-old granddaughter Tessa Garnett, Margie created a PowerPoint presentation about the memorial, which she used when the PRAC approved the project in August.

Funding and Site Planning

In addition to those developments, several fundraising ideas were exchanged at Betty Marriott's home, including that of a concert offered by Juneau violinist Steve Tada, whose own family in Seattle and Tokyo were devastated during World War II. Then in August 2012, the full Empty Chair Committee met for the first time, and on August 7, Margie gave her new PowerPoint presentation about the project to City and Borough of Juneau assembly members, and to everyone's relief, the site location was formally endorsed at that meeting. It was time to raise funds in earnest, and Roger, Andy Pekovich and David Gray began soliciting donations. However, despite no official fundraising kickoff, the community spontaneously and earnestly responded to presentations, radio programs and newspaper coverage, keeping Betty Marriott and Jan Pekovich busy writing committee thank yous to numerous donors.

In August, Peter visited Juneau to walk Capital School Park with then Juneau Parks and Recreation Director Brent Fischer and Parks Superintendent George Schaaf to view the site chosen by the committee. Peter said the memorial would be handicap accessible so that all visitors could circle it in order to read the names, text, and symbols on the memorial's base.

At an Empty Chair Committee meeting welcoming Peter, Roger showed him a small, wooden chair from his family's vintage 1930s cabin. It made such a hit with Peter that he took it back to Seattle to use as a model for the memorial. He wrote to the committee about his time in Juneau, "Right from the start of this project, it just felt right. The story is such a compelling one, and I'm honored to be a part of it. And now that I've been to Juneau, seen the site with my own eyes and met some of the people involved, I feel even more so that this project is a special one. The way you all have welcomed me into your circle of friends must be somewhat like the way the Japanese families must have felt on their return to the city. It's clear that there are a lot of caring and compassionate people there, and that's a real comfort. I'm looking forward to working with all of you throughout the life of this project." Peter planned to begin the project in July 2013.

Roger and I continued presentations to various organizations and particularly through Sharon Gaiptman and Kelly Peres at KINY/KJNO and Jeff Brown at public radio station KTOO. Eventually, as site planning progressed, the idea for siting the memorial atop the rise in the park moved to a more easily accessed spot below it and nearer the existing walkway. This change necessitated some kind of retaining structure that eventually transformed into a two-foot sitting wall; so Roger and I toured Juneau sites, researching walls and stone that would stand up to Juneau's harsh, wet climate.

Joe Yasutake of the Japanese American Museum of San Jose, California, learned of the Empty Chair Project from Alice and encouraged the committee to apply for a National Park Service Japanese American Confinement Sites Grant, which is designed specifically for the preservation and interpretation of sites where Japanese Americans were detained during World War II. With Yasutake's guidance, Margie and Mary, who had never written a grant application, completed theirs within the two-month September deadline. Since the Empty Chair Committee lacked nonprofit status, Juneau Parks and Recreation Director Brent Fischer agreed to be the National Park Service's local grant authorizing official for the project's application and administration.

In February 2013, Margie, Mary and Alice arrived in Juneau to attend a benefit concert with Steve Tada of

Juneau on violin and Nancy Nash of Haines, Alaska, on piano. The musicians chose pieces by Robert and Clara Schumann and Johannes Brahms for their connection to what they considered the concepts embodied in the Empty Chair Project. Nancy said, "Distressing things happen to people, but friendship and true community can help in healing from the pain." The Northern Lights Presbyterian Church waived the fee for the space, and the artists donated all receipts to the committee, which included a generous donation from the Gastineau Channel Historical Society. Mary said, "My sister and I were overwhelmed by the church filled with well-wishers who had come to hear the beautiful music and to show support for the project."

Steve Tada and Nancy Nash, benefit concert sponsors and musicians. (Courtesy of Steve Tada & Nancy Nash)

Also during that time, the Downtown Juneau Public Library hosted an informational panel. Organized by committee member Marsha Bennett, it featured Margie, Mary, Alice, and Randy Wanamaker, a Juneau Assembly member whose grandfather had been incarcerated. During the question and answer period, committee member Jackie Triplette asked the audience how many people had eaten at the City Café. The room erupted in smiles and raised hands of those who remembered the popular hangout for good food garnished with the sports and political repartee encouraged by Sam and Gim Taguchi.

The fundraising and donations of time, labor and materials likewise erupted. Memories of the City Café and the shock of discovering what had happened to their friends in 1942 added considerable energy to the project. The community was responding to the incarceration once again. Meanwhile, Mary and Jane Lindsey, Juneau-Douglas City Museum director, collaborated on an exhibit titled

Yes, they all ate at the City Café once upon a time. Downtown Juneau Library panel discussion. (Mary Abo photo)

The Forced Removal and Resettlement of Juneau's Japanese Community, 1941-1951. By August the exhibit, curated by Jodi DuBruyne with designs by Sarah Olsen, was slated for the summer to fall of 2014. It would feature first person narratives, photographs and artifacts of eight incarcerated Juneau families: Kiichi (Henry) Akagi, Hikohachi Fukuyama, Torao and Tooru Kanazawa, Saburo (Sam, Sr.) Kito, Katsutaro Komastsubara, Haruo Kamasaka, Sam and Gim Taguchi and Shonosuke Tanaka.

Roger, volunteering as site coordinator, began calling on contractors he had known during his years as an insurance broker. He asked his former high school classmate Jim Triplette of Triplette Construction for help with site development details. Jim in turn contacted his colleague Wayne Jensen of Jensen Yorba Lott, Inc.'s architectural firm, who volunteered to develop site plans, which were subsequently accepted by the city. Jim Williams, owner of North Pacific Erectors, told Roger, "I'd do anything for Sam Taguchi," and offered to ship the memorial from Seattle. Within a year, with the community's and donors' overwhelmingly generous response, along with the persistent fundraising by Roger, the Empty Chair Committee reached its goal to pay for the memorial, the first of its kind in Alaska.

Then, in July 2013, Margie received the extraordi-
nary news that the Empty Chair Project had qualified
for a Japanese American Confinement Sites grant in
the amount of $80,000 from the National Park Service.
However, the grant required a two-for-one match, meaning the project was required to contribute $40,000. This
was accomplished by supplying $26,000 from the project's
fundraising efforts and $14,000 from in-kind donations,
which increased the grant total to $120,000. On October
14, 2013, after reviewing the grant, the City and Borough
of Juneau Assembly approved an ordinance to appropri-
ate $106,000 for the project. This amount, along with the
$14,000 of in-kind donations, completed the grant require-
ment. In fact, due to the generosity of local businesses, the
total in-kind donations would far exceed this amount. All
funds and in-kind donations would be used for video/au-
dio interviews, site preparation and delivery, installation
of the memorial, and educational materials and activities
in schools, libraries and museums.

Roger continued to receive positive responses from
contractors. Jerry Godkin, Inc. offered to excavate the site.
Jim Triplette took on the job of constructing a sitting wall
form, placing it and coordinating the cement pour with
Bob Lupro of AGGPRO, who volunteered the cement. In
addition, Jim stored the memorial until it was placed at the
site. In fact, Jim coordinated all the labor and equipment
those details required, as well as coordinating placement
of Peter Reiquam's sculpture, all while still conducting his
own contracting business. Alaska Stone & Concrete provided the labor for placing the stone siding on the sitting
wall, and Jim Williams paid for the stone.

Site preparation started in May 2014 with removal of
sod by Roger and his former classmates Tom Blanton and
Joe Heueisen. On June 2, the site was excavated, on June
11 the sitting wall form was placed and the chair, barged
from Seattle though the generosity of Jim Williams, arrived
on June 17. The cement slab for the chair was poured

Site Construction

Jerry Godkin, Jr. excavates the memorial site in Capital School Park.

Roger Grummett and Jim Triplette consult onsite via cell phone with Peter Reiquam, memorial artist, in Seattle.

The large sitting wall form is moved to the excavated space.

Wall and cement pours are completed.

John Dybdahl and Peter drill a metal grid into cement for the memorial's base.

on June 19, and Peter arrived on June 25. The following morning, Triplette Construction's boom truck operator, John Dybdahl, brought the boxed chair to the memorial site where it was uncrated, and Peter and John attached metal brackets to the site's cement slab. Then, guided by Peter's hand signals, John, at the controls, gingerly moved the chair from the truck to the cement slab where they bolted the sculpture's base to the metal grid. After a little polishing by Peter, the chair was finally home. The crew covered the chair with the crate it came in until the dedication ceremony.

The Dedication

In Japanese culture, one thousand cranes can represent a form of healing, hope and peace during challenging times. Origami paper cranes, strung in various sizes and colors, are often placed at other Japanese American incarceration memorials. The idea to use paper cranes during the dedication gained support and soon a group, organized by Jackie Triplette, held origami crane-making workshops in Jackie's home and a public one at the Juneau-Douglas City Museum. In time, the crane crew completed 1,000 paper cranes for the dedication. Betty Marriott's friends contributed over 2,000 cranes, including Tina Kobayashi's 1,150 from Hawaii and Susan Oshida's string of 1,000. In addition, other Empty Chair committee members and supporters in such locations as Vermont and British Columbia contributed another 1,000. The cranes provided colorful additions to the museum's exhibit and various events, including local library displays, and long, colorful chains of them would cover the memorial before its formal unveiling at the dedication.

The dedication incorporated a weekend of events for the community and the 42 family members of former incarcerees who planned to attend. In the spirit of homecoming, all were greeted at Juneau International Airport

The Empty Chair Memorial Dedication

July 12, 2014, 2 p.m.
Capital School Park
Juneau, Alaska

平和

Opening Remarks, Introductions.....................Brent Fischer,
Department of Parks & Recreation Director, NPS Grant Administrator.
Mayor Merrill Sanford

Honored Guests.........................Marjorie Alstead Shackelford
Assisted by Karleen Alstead Grummett

Empty Chair Committee...........................Brent Fischer

Site Coordinator.............................Roger Grummett

Artist's Remarks..............................Peter Reiquam

Memorial Unveiling..........Gabryel Kito, Maya & Aiko Abo Dominguez,
Tessa & Zoe Garnett, Koen Schultz & Clare Homan. Assisted by Janie Homan.

Haru no Umi 春の海 "The Sea in Spring".............Steve Tada
Nancy Nash

Reading of the Memorial Narrative............Alice Tanaka Hikido

Reading of Honoree Names........Betty Echigo Marriott, Julie Abo,
Todd Albright & Jeff Tanaka

Reflections............................Marie Darlin, Walter Fukuyama

Furusato 故郷 "My Home Town"..........Kristi & Bethany Tanaka

平和

Cranes Coordinator: Jackie Triplette
Booklet/Program Ushers: Emma Tanaka, Emily Hikido, Amber
Tanaka, Alicia & Tyler Bianchetto, Mitchell Henderson & Stacy Grummett.

The chair is veiled with strands of origami paper cranes. (Gina Garnett photo)

Crowds fill Capital School Park for the dedication. (Marcelo Quinto photo)

Margie Shackelford, Empty Chair Project head, welcomes attendees and honorees.

(Gina Garnett photo)

A lighter moment: After Brent Fischer, Juneau's Parks and Recreation Director, National Parks Service grant authorizing official and master of ceremonies introduces the Empty Chair Committee, Roger Grummett acknowledges site contractors. (Marlena Sloss, *Juneau Empire*)

Sam Kito, Jr. takes his turn to be recognized as fellow honorees applaud. L. to R. Mary Abo, Randy Wanamaker, Walter Fukuyama, Alice Hikido, Sam Kito, Jr. (Marlena Sloss, *Juneau Empire* photo)

Peter Reiquam, memorial artist, gives his remarks. (Gina Garnett photo)

and escorted to town where welcome signs from the Juneau Convention and Visitors Bureau were displayed in business windows throughout the city. To kick off the weekend, Greg Chaney's film premiered on Friday, July 11 at the 20th Century Theatre, whose venue was donated by Gross Alaska Theaters. The premiere was followed by a welcoming reception for the honored guests. Sponsored by Shattuck and Grummett Insurance Inc., it was organized by committee member Janie Homan to occur at the Silverbow Inn where artist Joyce Mill provided the crane-themed table decorations. In addition, the Downtown Juneau Library featured a book display related to the incarceration.

The next day, post-dedication activities plans included a public reception hosted by the Juneau-Douglas City Museum where guests could view their family stories and artifacts on exhibit. In addition, tours of the former Juneau High School gym, located in the building where the actual 1942 graduation took place, would be provided by Alaska's Legislative Affairs staff, the agency now occupying the building. That evening, a final screening of Chaney's film, this time at the Gold Town Nickelodeon Theatre, would conclude the weekend's activities.

The memorial dedication took place on the rainy afternoon of July 12, 2014, four years to the day Margie and I sat in Betty Marriott's living room. Former incarcerees and family members gathered beneath protective awnings at Capital School Park. Jeanne Tanaka observed of the weather, "It's perfect," she said. "It's like a baptism." Over 300 people stood in the mist to witness the event honoring eight family representatives: Walter Fukuyama, Jeanne Tanaka, Alice Hikido, Mary Abo and Sam Kito, Jr. Randy Wanamaker representing his grandfather Henry Akagi. Lisa Taguchi, Gim Taguchi's daughter, and Reiko Sumada, Sam and Gim's sister (who was weather delayed), represented the Taguchi brothers, and Mike Tanaka represented his father, Bill Tanaka.

Honorees L. to R. Mary Abo, Randy Wanamaker, Walter Fukuyama, Alice Hikido, and Sam Kito, Jr. Young people brought each honoree a strand of origami cranes from the veiled chair. (Marlena Sloss, *Juneau Empire* photo)

Maya and Aiko Abo Dominguez

Karleen Grummett gives each honoree an origami crane pin and a hug. (Gina Garnett photo)

Todd Albright, Betty Marriott, Julie Abo and Jeff Tanaka speak the names of the incarcerated.

Honorees reflect as the names are called: Lisa Taguchi, daughter of Gim Taguchi and niece to Sam Taguchi; Jeanne Tanaka, wife of John Tanaka; Mike Tanaka, son of William "Bill" Tanaka. (Marlena Sloss, *Juneau Empire*)

The bronze chair sat veiled in its strands of colorful origami cranes as master of ceremonies Brent Fischer introduced Mayor Merrill Sanford. He welcomed everyone saying, "The citizens of Juneau are proud and honored to have this memorial in our home town" and were "humbled to accept the gift." Roger, Margie and Peter spoke about the community of friends who worked on the project and Juneau's astounding response. Margie said, "The original chair was placed as a silent protest of the forcible removal and incarceration of Juneau's Japanese community at the class of 1942's graduation. Our fervent hope is that this chair will remind future generations that, although we are sometimes powerless to prevent injustice, in the words of Elie Wiesel, a holocaust survivor, 'there should never be a time when we fail to protest it.'"

1943 classmates, Marie Darlin and Walter Fukuyama, respond to the dedication program. (Gina Garnett photo)

Margie introduced the eight honored guests, and Sam Kito, Jr.'s granddaughter Gabi explained the meaning of the cranes. "It is a Japanese custom that if you make 1,000 cranes, your wish will come true," Gabi said. "By covering the Empty Chair with these cranes, our community expresses a wish for peace, harmony and remembrance." Then grandchildren of former incarcerees and friends unveiled the chair's strands and laid them into the laps of each guest as Steve Tada, accompanied on keyboard by Nancy Nash, played his soulful violin rendition of "Haru no Umi" (The Sea in Spring). Alice read the memorial narrative, and Betty and incarceree family members read each name etched on the memorial's base.

As former classmates and friends Walter Fukuyama and Marie Darlin gave reflections about the 1942 special graduation, Walter said, "I'm really overwhelmed by this beautiful celebration, this Empty Chair, that the

City of Juneau, the Parks and Recreation Department and all these committee people…. that they could put something like this on. You know, they must have all had one heart and one spirit to do it, and I'm sure this is what happened." Bethany and Kristi Tanaka closed the dedication ceremony with a violin solo and reading of the lyrics to the Japanese song "Furusato" (Coming Home). Finally, some justice had been achieved.

The journey to establish the Empty Chair Memorial encompassed a determined number of people who were very aware that their generation was the last with an emotional connection to the incarceration event. They realized, if they didn't memorialize it, such a tribute might never happen. However, the project was a collaboration heavily influenced by sisters Alice Hikido and Mary Abo and all the Juneau Japanese and Tlingit families who shared their stories. But for their work, and the work of the Juneau community, this project would never have achieved the meaning it exemplifies.

Jeanne Tanaka spoke to that thought when she wrote in gratitude about The Empty Chair Memorial, which was prompted by her husband's story: "This will be a living legacy for the world to see, but especially for those who experienced the injustice, yet kept their faith, returned home and were welcomed back. It will bring back many memories, never forgotten, that are so ingrained and a part of us today. This is my personal acknowledgement of your thoughtful and kind way to memorialize the deepest meaning of a community."

Until fairly recently, many people born during and after the war, including those of Japanese ancestry, had never heard from their community, parents or schools about the forced removal. As Randy Wanamaker said of his grandfather, "I don't remember him or William (Randy's uncle) ever talking about the incarceration camps." Sam Kito, Jr. said, "My parents hardly talked about the family's internment experience except to say, "'It was a tough time.'" He and his daughter, Hope, recently made a pilgrimage to Minidoka. "She's glad we went together," he said, "and now we both know what it was like."

The committee's goal is that the Empty Chair Memorial serves as a symbol of justice for people of all generations who may learn and gain inspiration from the memorial site, which demonstrates the Nation's commitment to equal justice under the law. When Randy, Sam, Hope and all affected families visit the memorial, we hope they can take some small measure of comfort in Juneau's response to the incarceration.

> After Japan bombed Pearl Harbor on December 7, 1941, people of Japanese ancestry living on America's West Coast were forcibly removed and incarcerated in isolated government internment camps. In May 1942, the seniors at Juneau High School left an empty chair during their graduation ceremony to underscore the absence of their Japanese-American Valedictorian, John Tanaka. By extension, this empty chair honors all of the Japanese uprooted from their homes and communities. The Empty Chair Memorial represents the void the people of Juneau felt for their friends and neighbors impacted by this injustice. The names of those interned are etched on the bronze floor. A time may come when these names will be forgotten, but the symbol of the empty chair will remind future generations of the lessons learned from this compelling and poignant story.
>
> — Narrative on the Empty Chair Memorial.

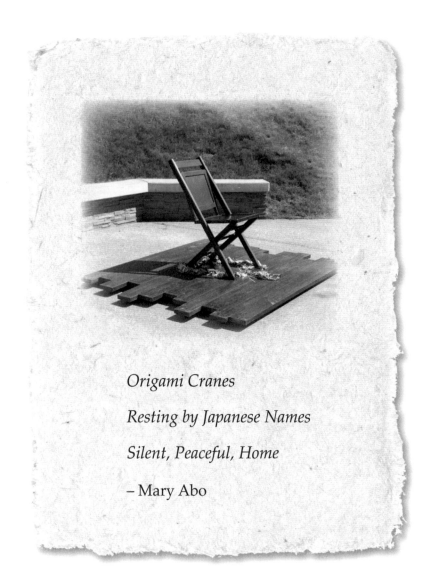

Origami Cranes

Resting by Japanese Names

Silent, Peaceful, Home

– Mary Abo

The Empty Chair Project

In addition to creating the Empty Chair Memorial, the project has also focused on educating others about the empty chair story. Under the coordination of the committee's educational advisor, Stephen McPhetres, who joined the committee in 2014, and along with the University of Alaska Southeast Lecture Series in Juneau, the project featured the Seattle-based Living Voices presentation of *Within the Silence*. The weekend event also included a display in the campus's Egan Library and a showing of Greg Chaney's documentary, *The Empty Chair*. *Within the Silence*, a unique solo performance combined with archival film that turns the history of Japanese incarceration into a moving, personal journey, was shown again at UAS in 2015 and to the Juneau School District's fifth grade students both years.

Stephen McPhetres

During this time, Steve, a former Alaska school administrator, assisted by his wife and former teacher, Jan, created and guided an Empty Chair Project education committee of Juneau incarcerees, teachers, city museum staff, and school and state librarians for the purpose of integrating the Juneau Japanese community's incarceration experience into the Juneau School District's fifth grade curriculum. The group received helpful resources and feedback from the staff of Sakai Intermediate School on Bainbridge Island, Washington, which has successfully incorporated their community's World War II incarceration stories into their social studies and language arts curriculum. To that end, the project's retired teachers Margie Shackelford and Mary Abo collected a variety of instructional materials, including texts, photos and DVDS about the incarceration, and created instructional kits based upon the Juneau-Douglas City Museum's exhibit *The Forced Removal and*

Notes from Juneau fifth graders to the Empty Chair Committee thanking them for showing *Within the Silence:*

"For so many people to be interned so harshly is very sad! For me, realizing this happened was surprising and did change my way of thinking."

"Thank you for telling our community this story. I know that it will now be remembered and respected among the Juneau people."

"I like to think that my generation will not even think about doing it again. So I thank you. I still can't believe such a terrible thing even took place."

Resettlement of Juneau's Japanese Community 1941-1951. These materials are now available to all schools in the Juneau School District.

Since the Empty Chair Memorial's dedication, the project's efforts have been honored. In 2014, it received recognition from the Alaska Historical Society with the Esther Billman Certificate of Excellence Award for contributing to the preservation and understanding of Alaskan history. In 2015, the Alaska State Legislature honored the project with a citation, sponsored by Representative Sam Kito, Jr. and signed by 49 other Alaska representatives, for the Empty Chair Committee's work. That was followed by national recognition of Peter Reiquam's Empty Chair Memorial sculpture as an outstanding public art project by Americans for the Arts, a national nonprofit focused on advancing the arts and arts education.

In June 2015, the National Park Service's Minidoka National Historic Site in Idaho featured an Empty Chair exhibit and presentation during the site's annual pilgrimage program. To preserve the 2014 Juneau-Douglas City Museum exhibit for educational purposes, the project, under Mary Abo's direction, had photos and narratives digitally transferred onto retractable banners, which were displayed at the pilgrimage and other NPS events. Later that year, two final pieces were added to the memorial: A bronze plaque, donated by Alan and Lisa Akiyama, son and daughter of the late Dr. Henry I. and Grace E. Akiyama of Juneau, and a project-sponsored interpretive sign giving historical information about the memorial. The site is also featured in the Juneau Convention and Visitors Bureau and Juneau Arts and Humanities Council walking maps and in the comprehensive annual travel guide, *Alaska Milepost*.

In April 2016, Greg Chaney's award-winning documentary, *The Empty Chair*, which has been viewed at several film festivals outside of Alaska, was featured at the Japanese American National Museum in Los Angeles. The film is responsible for bringing the Empty Chair's story to a wider audience. Also in 2016, the project sponsored two authors whose books depict stories connected to the Japanese incarceration. Jamie Ford wrote the bestselling novel *Hotel on the Corner of Bitter and Sweet*, a Seattle-based story about love and friendship between a Chinese American boy and a Japanese American girl. Kirby Larson's book, *Dash*, which received a Newbery Honor, is the moving story of a Japanese-American girl who is separated from her dog upon being sent to an incarceration camp. Both authors spent most of their time in Juneau giving workshops at local schools.

To ensure that the efforts of the Empty Chair Project are preserved, the Alaska State Historical Library is in the process of creating a website for all Empty Chair documents, photos, videotaped interviews, transcripts and other historical information associated with the incarceration of Japanese Alaskans. More information about the Empty Chair Project can be found at the project's website www.emptychairproject.wordpress.com.

The Empty Chair Committee
Juneau, Alaska

L. to R. Back Row: Margie Shackelford, Janie Homan, Andy Pekovich, Dixie Belcher, Roger Grummett, Marsha Bennett, Karleen Grummett, advisors Greg Chaney & Jim Triplette. Front Row: Jan Pekovich, Jackie Triplette, Betty Marriott & Marie Darlin.

Advisor Brent Fischer, NPS grant authorizing official.

Ron Inouye, Alaska Japanese history advisor. *(See advisor Stephen McPhetres, p. 158).*

David Gray.

Committee members Alice Hikido, left, and Mary Abo, right, shown with their sister-in-law, Jeanne (John) Tanaka. (Jim Tanaka photo)

Sources

"Air Transportation. Alaska's Heritage." *Alaska History and Cultural Studies*. Alaska Humanities Forum. Web. Retrieved January 2015 http://www.akhistorycourse. org/articles/article.php?artID=177

"Alaska Japs to Report to Army for Evacuation." *Daily Alaska Empire* 20 Apr. 1942: 1+

"Alaska Jap Evacuees Go to Puyallup." *Daily Alaska Empire* 23 Apr. 19.

Alaska Labor and Workforce Development Dept., Research & Development Division, 1880-2000 Census Data. Web. Retrieved Feb. 2015 < http://labor.alaska.gov/research/census/hist.htm>

Albright, Nancy. Transcribed quote from taped interview of Tom Fukuyama by his son Keith. Message to author, 4 March 2015.

"Boy, Girl are 1st Births in Camp. *Camp Harmony News Letter*. 23 May 1942. Web. Retrieved Dec. 2014 <http://www.lib.washington.edu/exhibits/harmony/Newsletter/1-4.html>

Blanchard, Morgan. Senior Archaeologist, Northern Land Use Research Alaska, LLC. Email to author 12 June 2015.

Buchholdt, Thelma. "Filipino American History Timeline." 1 Jan. 1999. Web. Retrieved 13 Feb. 2015 <http://www.fanhs17.com/timeline.htm>

Cooley, Adrienne. Note to Marie Darlin. 2012

Davis, Trevor. *Looking Back on Juneau, the first hundred years: a pictorial memorabilia*. Juneau, AK: Miner Publishing Co., 1979, 247.

Fujioka, Shirou. *Ayumi No Ato* (Footprints in the Past). Los Angeles: Kengorou Nakamura/Rafu Shimp, 1957, 408-409.

Fukuyama, Walter. Interview recorded by Greg Chaney. 8 June 2013. Seattle. DVD.

Fukuyama, Walter. Letter to his father Hikohachi Fukuyama. 6 June 1943. MS.

Fukuyama, Walter T. NVC Foundation Japanese American Memorial Wall. Web. Retrieved 23 Mar. 2013 http://nvcmemorialwall.org

Fukuyama, Walter and Ethel Fukuyama Terashita. Transcribed interview by Carol Hoshiko for Alaska's Japanese Pioneers Research Project. 17 May 1991. Seattle.

Hara, Kimi and friends. "Tsamu "Sam" Taguchi." *Gastineau Channel Memories 1880-1967 Vol. II.* Juneau: 2004. 381-382.

Griffiths, Melissa. "The empty chair and a hushed history." *Juneau Empire* 6 May 2012.

Griffiths, Melissa. "Moving Forward with Looking Back." *Juneau Empire*. 12 August 2012: C+

Hikido, Alice Tanaka. *In the Same Boat*. California of the Past Digital Storytelling Project. San Leandro Public Library, CA. 2011.

Hikido, Alice Tanaka. "Shonosuke and Nobu Tanaka." *Gastineau Channel Memories 1880-1959*. Juneau: 2001. 499-500.

Hikido, Alice Tanaka. Interview by Greg Chaney and Ron Inouye 9 June 2013. Bremerton, WA. Transcribed and edited by Jeff Tanaka and Mary Abo.

Hurley, Katie Torkelsen. *The Empty Chair*. Documentary by Greg Chaney. DVD. 2014.

"Ideal Farewell Gift Presented B. Tanaka by Nine Classmates."*J-Bird* 24 Apr. 1942: 3.

"Images from another time: Juneau icon, 1989." Caption of Sam Taguchi. *Juneau Empire* 26 July 2006.

Inouye, Ron, Carol Hoshiko and Kazumi Heshiki. *Alaska's Japanese Pioneers Faces, Voices, Stories. Alaska Pioneers Research Project*. Fairbanks: 1994.

Inouye, Ron. "Little known story of Alaska Issei." *Pacific Citizen* 5 October 1984: 11-12.

"John Tanaka Gets Diploma Today at JHS."
Daily Alaska Empire 15 Apr. 1942.

"John Tanaka is in Eden, Idaho." *J-Bird*. 30 Oct. 1942: 4.

Kanazawa, Tooru. *Sushi and Sourdough*. Seattle: University of
Washington Press, 1989.

Kashima, Tetsuden. *Judgement without Trial: Japanese American
Imprisonment during World War II*. Seattle: University of
Washington Press, 2003.

Kito, Sam II. Videotaped interview by Greg Chaney and Ron
Inouye 31 Jan. 2014. Juneau City Hall Conference Room.
Transcribed by Ron Inouye Feb. 2014.

Kumasaka, Ham. Interview recorded by Greg Chaney 8 June
2013. Interviewers: Greg Chaney, Ron Inouye, Alice
Hikido, Mary Abo. Seattle. DVD.

"Mary Fukuyama Studying in Japan." *J-Bird* 8 March 1940: 1.

Metcalfe, Vern. "Tanaka Death." *Juneau Empire* Letter to the
Editor. 1977.

"Minidoka." National Park Service, U. S. Dept. of the Interior,
National Historic Site, Jerome, ID. Undated leaflet,
June 2015.

Minidoka Interlude: September 1942-October 1943. Published by
residents of Minidoka Relocation Center, Hunt, Idaho.

Murray, Leslie. "Some local citizens spent war years in
internment camps." *Juneau Empire*. Undated.

Naske, Claus-M. "The Relocation of Alaska's Japanese
Residents." *Pacific Northwest Quarterly* 74.3 (1983):
128 & 132.

Nash, Nancy. "Note from Nancy." The Empty Chair Project
website, March 2013 archive. Retrieved Feb. 2016.
http://emptychairproject.wordpress.com

National Personnel Records Center. "Enlisted Record and
Report of Separation" listing the honorable discharge of
John Tanaka and sent to Mary Abo 8 December 2014.

Okubo, Miné. *Citizen 13660.* New York City: Columbia
University Press, 1946.

Oswald, Erling. Family history submitted to Janet Ruotsala. 17 Jan. 2001.

Pohl, Jeanine. "Remembering Sam: Serving up politics or hash browns, Sam Taguchi was a diner institution." *Juneau Empire*. Undated.

"Proceedings of a Board of Civilians in the Case of Shonosuke Tanaka, Japanese Enemy Alien." Juneau: 9 January 1942. Tanaka family document.

Reefe, Pat, Nancy Stephenson and Rose Wayne. "Katsutaro and Rose (Oyama) Komatsubara." *Gastineau Channel Memories 1880-1967, Vol. II.* Juneau: 2004.

"Relocation of Japanese Americans." War Relocation Authority, Washington, D. C., May 1943. The Virtual Museum of the City of San Francisco web. Retrieved Aug. 2015 http://www.sfmuseum.org/hist10/relocbook.html

Ripley, Rudy. "Sam Taguchi will be missed by all." For *Juneau Empire* 1995.

Sato, Kenichi. 1996 Distinguished Alumnus Award Citation for John M. Tanaka, M.D., 1924-1978. University Students Club, Inc., University of Washington, Seattle.

Schoenfeld, Ed. "Pioneer 'Sim' MacKinnon Dies." *Juneau Empire* 2 Aug. 1990.

Shackelford, Marjorie Alstead. Empty Chair Dedication Speech. 12 July 2014.

"Southeast Alaska State Parks." Division of Parks and Outdoor Recreation. State of Alaska web. Retrieved January 2015 <https://openlibrary.org/books/OL2212559M/Sushi_and_sourdough>

Stone, David and Brenda. *Hard Rock Gold.* Juneau: City and Borough of Juneau, Juneau Centennial Committee, 1980.

Taguchi, Sam. A transcribed interview by Ron Inouye for Alaska's Japanese Pioneers Research Project. 19 and 20 Oct. 1990. Juneau: Alaska Historical Library.

Taguchi, Takeshi "Gim." Obituary. *Juneau Empire* 10 June 1997: 2.

Tanaka, Jeanne Aoyama. Videotaped interview by Greg Chaney. Edited by Mary Abo and Jeff Tanaka, transcribed by Jeff Tanaka. 10 June 2013. Seattle.

Tanaka, Jeff. *The Empty Chair Project Memorial Dedication.* 12 July 2013. DVD. Retrieved 12 June 2015 <https://www.youtube.com/watch?v=tl_8Mqk6Boo>

Tanaka, Jeff. Nikkei Memories blog. Mary Abo quote. Retrieved 22 Aug. 2015 https://www.nikkeimemories.tumblr.com

Tanaka, John. Letter to General Simon D. Buckner, Alaskan Defense Command, Anchorage, AK 3 Apr. 1943 with five sworn affidavits of Juneau businessmen to his father's loyalty to the United States.

"Tanaka Presented Diploma at Unique Graduation April 15." *J Bird* 24 Apr. 1942: 1.

Tanaka, Shonosuke. Letter to Edward J. Ennis, Director, Enemy Alien Control Unit, Department of Justice, Washington, D. C. 4 asking for discharge from parole. 4 December 1945.

Tanaka, William "Bill" Tanaka. Transcribed interview by Mary Tanaka Abo. 9 Nov. 1996. San Pedro, CA.

Terashita, Ethel Fukuyama. "Walter and Mume Fukuyama." *Gastineau Channel Memories 1880-1959.* Juneau, 2001: 165-167.

Wanamaker, Randy Akagi. Interview by Greg Chaney and transcribed by Mary Abo and Jeff Tanaka. January 2014. Juneau.

Weather Forecast Office, U. S. National Weather Service, Juneau, AK. Downtown weather data for Apr 1942 and Dec. 1941. Retrieved 3 Oct. 2012 and 5 Sept. 2013.

WESTERN DEFENSE COMMAND AND FOURTH ARMY
Office of Assistant Chief of Staff, Civil Affairs Division

WARTIME CIVIL CONTROL ADMINISTRATION
1231 MARKET STREET
SAN FRANCISCO, CALIFORNIA
Telephone KLONDIKE 2-2611

January 30, 1943

MEMORANDUM FOR: Major M. H. Astrup

SUBJECT: Aleutians who were included in evacuation from
                   West Coast military areas.

In response to the undated air mail memorandum from Mr.
E. R. Fryer to you, we are transmitting herewith:

1. A complete list of Alaskan Japanese who have
   been turned over to the Immigration and Naturaliza-
   tion Service for internment, showing in each case
   the ISN serial number and the place of apprehension.

2. A complete list of Alaskan Japanese evacuated to
   the United States and transferred to War Relocation
   Centers, showing in each case sex, age, former
   Alaskan residence and present location.

It is thought that Mr. Fryer may be able to pick from these
two lists, persons specifically from the Aleutian Islands in which
he is particularly interested.

Calvert L. Dedrick
Chief, Statistical Division

Attachments (3)
  1-Memo from Mr. Fryer to
     Major Astrup
  2-List, Japanese Alaskan
     Internees
  3-List, Japanese Alaskan
     Evacuees

31.035

First Incarcerated Japanese Alaskans (Page 1)

(1) Males:

Name	Serial Number	Apprehended at:
Akagi, Kirichi	ISN AJ 1309 CI	Killisnoo X
Akimoto, Naoyoshi	ISN AJ 1 CI	Seward
Aoto, Asakeito	ISN AJ 1310 CI	Killisnoo
Emori, Jinji	ISN AJ 1000 CI	SS Wilhemina (Chiyedamura Ouragun Gunbaken, Japan)
Eyon, John	ISN AJ 1404 CI	Wrangell
Foode, Tom	ISN AJ 608 CI	Cordova
Fujii, Ginichi	ISN AJ 500 CI	Fairbanks
Fujita, Tom	ISN AJ 1415 CI	Wrangell
Fukuyama, Wada H.	ISN AJ 1501 CI	Juneau
Hagiwara, Chokichi	ISN AJ 1435 CI	Ketchikan
Hama, Fred	ISN AJ 612 CI	Seward
Hama, Hideo	ISN AJ 5 CI	Seward
Hama, Tom M.	ISN AJ 611 CI	Seward
Haruki, Foy Haruzo	ISN AJ 2 CI	Anchorage
Heyano, John	ISN AJ 17 CI	Ekuk
Hikiji, Hikie	ISN AJ 15 CI	Anchorage
Hirotsuka, Joe	ISN AJ 19 CI	Ekuk
Ikegami, Joe E.	ISN AJ 1428 CI	Ketchikan
Inouye, Hakuio H.	ISN AJ 1509 CI	Juneau
Ito, George	ISN AJ 1600 CI	Kotzebue
Ito, Shikanosko	ISN AJ 1514 CI	Juneau
Kaino, S.	ISN AJ 1421 CI	Petersburg
Kajina, Tony	ISN AJ 1437 CI	Ketchikan
Kamimura, Hoyzo Jack	ISN AJ 1432 CI	Ketchikan
Kanazawa, Torao Bob	ISN AJ 1510 CI	Juneau
Kaneko, Takami	ISN AJ 6 CI	Seward
Kato, T.	ISN AJ 1306 CI	Sitka
Kawabe, Sotoro Harry	ISN AJ 3 CI	Seward
Kawata, S.	ISN AJ 1413 CI	Wrangell
Kazawa, Utaka	ISN AJ 1508 CI	Juneau
Kijike, Gora	ISN AJ 1434 CI	Ketchikan
Kimura, Jijiro	ISN AJ 1433 CI	Ketchikan
Kimura, Harry Yusuke	ISN AJ 13 CI	Anchorage
Kimura, Shijiro	ISN AJ 1001 CI	SS Wilhemina (Shanghai, China)
Kito, Saburo	ISN AJ 1411 CI	Petersburg
Kito, Tom	ISN AJ 1409 CI	Petersburg
Koda, Fred	ISN AJ 502 CI	Fairbanks
Komatsubara, K.	ISN AJ 1408 CI	Petersburg
Kono, Takashi	ISN AJ 1507 CI	Juneau

First Incarcerated Japanese Alaskans (Page 2)

Name	Serial Number	Apprehended at:
Kuwamoto, Torihei H.	ISN AJ 1513 CI	Juneau
Matsubayashi, Kojiro	ISN AJ 1512 CI	Juneau
Matsuoka, Martin	ISN AJ 804 CI	Kodiak
Mayeda, Henry	ISN AJ 1305 CI	Sitka
Miyasuto, George	ISN AJ 1419 CI	Wrangell
Mori, Tom	ISN AJ 1301 CI	Sitka
Moriuchi, Toyojiro	ISN AJ 1515 CI	Juneau
Moriyama, Etso	ISN AJ 1425 CI	Ketchikan
Moto, George	ISN AJ 1602 CI	Deering
Muyeyasu, Jim	ISN AJ 18 CI	Ekuk
Murata, Frank	ISN AJ 1304 CI	Sitka
Nakagawa, Harry	ISN AJ 504 CI	Tanana
Nakaike, Frank	ISN AJ 506 CI	Fairbanks
Nishiyama, George	ISN AJ 4 CI	Seward
Ohashi, Buck	ISN AJ 1438 CI	Ketchikan
Okegawa, Harry	ISN AJ 1406 CI	Petersburg
Omura, Roy Minoru	ISN AJ 1302 CI	Sitka
Osawa, Esaburo	ISN AJ 1414 CI	Petersburg
Oshima, George	ISN AJ 505 CI	Beaver
Oyama, Harushi	ISN AJ 1422 CI	Petersburg
Oyamada, Harry	ISN AJ 1436 CI	Ketchikan
Sakagami, Kisaku	ISN AJ 1420 CI	Petersburg
Sakamoto, C. L.	ISN AJ 1416 CI	Petersburg
Sakamoto, Harry	ISN AJ 1412 CI	Petersburg
Samoto, Harry	ISN AJ 1308 CI	Killisnoo
Sato, Torakichi	ISN AJ 14 CI	Anchorage
Shibata, Unosuke	ISN AJ 1417 CI	Wrangell
Shimizu, Katsui	ISN AJ 1426 CI	Ketchikan
Shimizu, Paul	ISN AJ 1506 CI	Juneau
Shiota, Yakei	ISN AJ 1517 CI	Juneau
Shirai, Harry	ISN AJ 1423 CI	Ketchikan
Sugeta, Ginichi	ISN AJ 1410 CI	Petersburg
Sumi, Tony	ISN AJ 16 CI	Bethel
Suzuki, George K.	ISN AJ 1402 CI	Ketchikan
Takenaka, Gaichi	ISN AJ 607 CI	Valdez
Takiguchi, George	ISN AJ 1405 CI	Wrangell
Tamaki, George	ISN AJ 1518 CI	Juneau
Tanaka, Shonosuke	ISN AJ 1502 CI	Juneau
Tanino, James M.	ISN AJ 1424 CI	Ketchikan
Tatsuda, James K.	ISN AJ 1403 CI	Ketchikan
Tayokawa, Toraichi	ISN AJ 1516 CI	Juneau
Togo, Zenji	ISN AJ 1427 CI	Ketchikan
Ura, Asakitchi	ISN AJ 1303 CI	Sitka
Urata, Ryataro	ISN AJ 1418 CI	Wrangell
Wada, George	ISN AJ 1511 CI	Juneau
Wada, Keizo	ISN AJ 1300 CI	Sitka
Watanabe, Fiso	ISN AJ 606 CI	Valdez
Yamada, George	ISN AJ 803 CI	Kodiak
Yamada, Kai	ISN AJ 1400 CI	Ketchikan
Yamamoto, Hiyo Frank	ISN AJ 1500 CI	Juneau
Yamauchi, Kuai	ISN AJ 609 CI	Cordova
Yasuda, Frank	ISN AJ 503 CI	Beaver
Yokoyama, C.	ISN AJ 1407 CI	Petersburg
Nakamura, Masaki	ISN AJ 1519 CI	Juneau

(2) Females:

Hama, Hisako	ISN AJ 610 CI	Seward
Kawabe, Tomo	ISN AJ 7 CI	Seward

Japanese Alaskan Family Incarcerees (Page 1)

JAPANESE ALASKAN EVACUEES

Name	Sex	Age	Residence	Present W.R.A.
Abe, George Jiro	M	29	Sitka	Minidoka 8/30/42
Akagi, William	M	26	Angoon	Minidoka 8/30/42
Dorkes, Heso	M	62	Tanakee Springs	Minidoka 8/30/42
Fujito, Katherine	F	20	Wrangell	Minidoka 8/30/42
, Lutes	F	21	Wrangell	Minidoka 8/30/42
Fukuyama, Ethel	F	19	Juneau	Minidoka 8/30/42
, Mume	F	49	Juneau	Minidoka 8/30/42
, Thomas	M	14	Juneau	Minidoka 8/30/42
, Walter	M	16	Juneau	Minidoka 8/30/42
Foods, Charles	M	24	Cordova	Minidoka 8/30/42
, George	M	27	Cordova	Minidoka 8/30/42
, John	M	29	Cordova	Minidoka 8/30/42
, Thomas	M	18	Cordova	Minidoka 8/30/42
Hagiwara, Michael	M	21	Ketchikan	Minidoka 8/30/42
, Shina	F	53	Ketchikan	Minidoka 8/30/42
Hayano, John, Jr.	M	9	Clarks Point	Minidoka 8/30/42
, Peter	M	19	Clarks Point	Minidoka 8/30/42
Hiratsuka, Frank	M	18	Clarks Point	Minidoka 8/30/42
, Mark	M	21	Clarks Point	Minidoka 8/30/42
, Thomas	M	23	Clarks Point	Minidoka 8/30/42
Hope, Henry	M	18	Wiseman	Minidoka 8/30/42
Imada, Katsura	M	19	Seward	Minidoka 8/30/42
Itubishi, Thomas	M	35	Juneau	Minidoka 8/30/42
Kuwata, William	M	11	Wrangell	Minidoka 8/30/42
Kaino, Frank	M	12	Petersburg	Minidoka 8/30/42
, Hanna	F	42	Petersburg	Minidoka 8/30/42
Kuwashima, Frances	F	20	Petersburg	Tule Lake 8/25/42
, Yoshio	M	27	Petersburg	Tule Lake 8/25/42
Kimura, Ben	M	16	Ketchikan	Minidoka 8/30/42
, Bert	M	19	Ketchikan	Minidoka 8/30/42
, Florence	F	14	Ketchikan	Minidoka 8/30/42
, Kagano	F	44	Ketchikan	Minidoka 8/30/42
, Martha	F	13	Ketchikan	Minidoka 8/30/42
, Masato	M	28	Anchorage	Minidoka 8/29/42
, Yukino	F	20	Anchorage	Minidoka 8/29/42
, George (Mrs.)	F	23	Anchorage	Minidoka 8/30/42
, Kitauyo	F	49	Anchorage	Minidoka 8/30/42
, Louise	F	24	Anchorage	Minidoka 8/30/42
, Sam	M	13	Anchorage	Minidoka 8/30/42
Kito, Amelia	F	23	Petersburg	Minidoka 8/30/42
, Barbara	F	3	Petersburg	Minidoka 8/30/42
, John	M	1	Petersburg	Minidoka 8/30/42
, Sam	M	5	Petersburg	Minidoka 8/30/42
Kumisaka, Haruo	M	23	Juneau	Minidoka 9/12/42
Komatsubara, Kiyoko	F	1	Petersburg	Minidoka 8/30/42
, Mitsuko	F	10 mo.	Petersburg	Minidoka 8/30/42
, Shizuka	F	5	Petersburg	Minidoka 8/30/42
, Tsuyo	F	37	Petersburg	Minidoka 8/30/42
Kuwata, Dick	M	12	Petersburg	Tule Lake 8/25/42
, June	F	8	Petersburg	Tule Lake 8/25/42
, Susie	F	16	Petersburg	Tule Lake 8/25/42
, Tsuyo	F	48	Petersburg	Tule Lake 8/25/42
Matsuda, Maseo Fred	M	23	Cordova	Minidoka 9/4/42
Matsuno, Fred	M	33	Pilot Point	Minidoka 8/30/42
Minamihata, Kahei	M	67	Ketchikan	Minidoka 9/3/42
Minemo, James	M	78	Wiseman	Died 6/5/42
Miyagawa, Frank	M	26	Fairbanks	Minidoka 8/30/42
, Hiromi	M	20	Fairbanks	Minidoka 8/30/42
, Mitsuye	F	22	Fairbanks	Minidoka 8/30/42
Miyasato, George	M	16	Wrangell	Minidoka 8/30/42
Mori, Takao (Mac)	M	28	Juneau	Minidoka 8/19/42
Moto, Donald	M	26	Deering	Minidoka 8/30/42
, James	M	33	Deering	Minidoka 8/30/42
, Taylor	M	31	Deering	Minidoka 8/30/42
Mukai, Thomas	M	28	Juneau	Minidoka 8/30/42
Nakamura, Mac	M	16	Juneau	Minidoka 8/30/42

Japanese Alaskan Family Incarcerees (Page 2)

Name	Sex	Age	Residence	Present W.R.A.
Nakashima, Yoneo	M	24	Ketchikan	Minidoka 8/30/42
Nishimoto, Francis	M	30	Seward	Minidoka 8/30/42
Noritake, Haruko	F	15	Ketchikan	Minidoka 8/30/42
, Masako	F	38	Ketchikan	Minidoka 8/30/42
Ohashi, Edward	M	10	Ketchikan	Minidoka 8/30/42
, Hope	F	13	Ketchikan	Minidoka 8/30/42
, Komatsu	F	36	Ketchikan	Minidoka 8/30/42
, Neil	M	12	Ketchikan	Minidoka 8/30/42
, Paul	M	8	Ketchikan	Minidoka 8/30/42
, Robert	M	16	Ketchikan	Minidoka 8/30/42
Okegawa, Darlene	F	1½	Petersburg	Minidoka 9/1/42
, George	M	21	Petersburg	Minidoka 9/1/42
, Georgiana	F	5 mo.	Petersburg	Minidoka 9/1/42
, Irene	F	19	Petersburg	Minidoka 9/1/42
Osawa, George	M	11	Petersburg	Minidoka 8/30/42
, Jiro	M	13	Petersburg	Minidoka 8/30/42
, Lilly	F	7	Petersburg	Minidoka 8/30/42
, Taka	F	45	Petersburg	Minidoka 8/30/42
Oyama, Seki	F	55	Petersburg	Minidoka 8/30/42
, Tsuruko	F	15	Petersburg	Minidoka 8/30/42
Ozawa, Henry	M	21	Sitka	Minidoka 8/30/42
, Joseph	M	24	Sitka	Minidoka 8/30/42
, Ivy	F	18	Sitka	Chinook, Mon. 6/5/42
, Paul	M	27	Sitka	Chinook, Mon. 6/5/42
Sakamoto, Uma	M	73	Sitka	Minidoka 8/29/42
Samato, William	M	27	Angoon	Minidoka 8/29/42
Sato, Mable	F	14	Anchorage	Minidoka 8/29/42
, William	M	17	Anchorage	Minidoka 8/30/42
Shimizu, Helen	F	22	Ketchikan	Minidoka 8/30/42
, Yayo	F	52	Ketchikan	Minidoka 8/30/42
Shirai, Harvey	M	31	Ketchikan	Minidoka 8/31/42
, Harvey, Jr.	M	4	Ketchikan	Manzanar 9/6/42
, James	M	2	Ketchikan	Pierce Co. Hospital Tacoma, Washington
, Minnie	F	24	Ketchikan	Mt. View Hospital Lake View, Wash.
, Rachel	F	1	Ketchikan	Manzanar 8/28/42
Suzuki, Edith	F	27	Ketchikan	Minidoka 8/30/42
, Howard	M	15	Ketchikan	Minidoka 8/30/42
, Tsuya	F	47	Ketchikan	Minidoka 8/30/42
Taguchi, Sam	M	24	Juneau	Minidoka 8/16/42
Tanaka, Alice	F	9	Juneau	Minidoka 8/30/42
, John	M	18	Juneau	Minidoka 8/30/42
, Nobu	F	37	Juneau	Minidoka 8/30/42
, Teruko	M	2	Juneau	Minidoka 8/30/42
, William	M	15	Juneau	Minidoka 8/30/42
Tanaka, Saburo	M	31	Juneau	Minidoka 8/30/42
Tanino, George	M	4	Ketchikan	Minidoka 8/30/42
, Henry	M	8	Ketchikan	Minidoka 8/30/42
, Hide	F	42	Ketchikan	Minidoka 8/30/42
, Hide	F	11	Ketchikan	Minidoka 8/30/42
, James	M	15	Ketchikan	Minidoka 8/30/42
, John	M	13	Ketchikan	Minidoka 8/30/42
, William	M	16	Ketchikan	Minidoka 8/30/42
Tatsuda, Billy	M	25	Ketchikan	Minidoka 8/30/42
, Kozu	F	24	Ketchikan	Minidoka 8/30/42
, Cherry	F	21	Ketchikan	Minidoka 8/30/42

In Appreciation

This book is a compilation from many sources and involved help from many people, including Jim Simard and his accommodating staff at the Alaska State Historical Library. Greg Chaney's interviews for his award-winning documentary, *The Empty Chair,* revealed new information, and he willingly shared the resulting DVD and taped interviews.

I was also able to glean insights from the first-person narratives included in the Juneau-Douglas City Museum exhibit, *The Empty Chair: The Forced Removal and Resettlement of Juneau's Japanese Community 1941-1951,* which ran from June to October 2014. In addition, I value the recollections shared by Bill Ray, Kim Metcalfe, Bill Ruddy, Dean Williams, Dennis P. Harris, Jane MacKinnon, Katherine Bavard Traeger, Al Shaw, John Dapcevich, Roberta Messerschmidt Spartz, Harry Sperling, William "Bill" Overstreet and Marie Darlin, who shared her own files and pointed the way to other resources.

In particular, I am indebted to Alice Tanaka Hikido for sharing her experiences and her family history through voluminous correspondence and conversation. Both Alice and her sister, Mary, shared priceless family photographs and documents, making research a much easier process.

I am especially thankful to my readers for their insights, questions and help: Kara Miyagishima, Ron Inouye, Alice Hikido, Mary Abo, Marjorie Shackelford, Beatrice Franklin, Nancy Olson, Marie Darlin, Dixie Belcher, Nancy Albright, and Don Cecil, who hears the commas. —kg